Triangulations within the Italy-Canada-United States Borderlands

Edited by

Luisa Del Giudice

BORDIGHERA PRESS
NEW YORK, NEW YORK

Robert Viscusi Essay Series
Volume 2

This series is dedicated to the long essay. It intends to publish studies that are longer than the traditional journal-length essay and yet shorter than the traditional book-length manuscript.

ISBN 978-1-59954-164-8
Library of Congress Control Number: 2020931271

© 2020 The Authors
All rights reserved
Printed in the United States of America

BORDIGHERA PRESS
John D. Calandra Italian American Institute
25 West 43rd Street, 17th Floor
New York, NY 10038

TABLE OF CONTENTS

Luisa Del Giudice, *Introduction* (v)

Giovanna Del Negro, *Never Canadian Enough: Chronic Otherness and Working-Class Cosmopolitanism in the Experience of an Immigrant Academic* (1)

Pasquale Verdicchio, *Photographic and Filmic Images of Cultural Triangulation* (29)

Luisa Del Giudice, *Evolving Triangulations within the Italy-Canada-United States Borderlands* (41)

CONTRIBUTORS (71)

Index of Names (75)

Introduction

TRIANGULATIONS WITHIN THE ITALY-CANADA-USA BORDERLANDS

Luisa Del Giudice

These essays had their origin in a panel I organized for the annual meeting of the Italian American Studies Association, held at the University of Toronto, Canada, from October 16-18, 2014: Academics in the Canada-Italy-US Borderlands. The panel included the authors in this volume, Pasquale Verdicchio, Giovanna Del Negro, and me, and reflected on the transnational identities of academics who straddled three boundaries, specifically those between post-World War II Italy, Canada, and the U.S.A., and how these life experiences had shaped their perspectives as academics in an increasingly borderless world. The panel reflected on the life and work of three academics (university-affiliated and independent) who had effectively straddled the divide, bringing an intimate consciousness of multiple national identities to bear on their research and writing, while engaging in research in all three nations.

When my alma mater was announced as the location of that meeting, my response was, dare I say, *triangular*. 1. Was the fact that a meeting on Italian *American* studies was being held in Canada yet another example of U.S. cultural imperialism?[1] (During the America-shunning days of my youth we bitterly complained of the unrequited love between neighbors: e.g., *we* were required to study U.S. history while Americans knew nothing about their northern neighbors. Alas, such asymmetries have not much wavered.); 2. Was our location meant to consciously enact the conference theme of diasporic transnational border crossings? 3. And finally, what did I and other Canadian-American-Italian members of our association, IASA, who for decades had dwelled intimately in these borderlands, have to say about our triadic loyalties? I knew that our contributions, as inter- and intra-continental scholars, operating within this specific triangle, would be unique, as we shared personal and scholarly reflections on our own various diasporic border crossings. We also represented a Canadian geographic (provincial) spectrum: from Verdicchio's Pacific-rim Vancouver (British Columbia) affiliation on the West coast, to my Anglophone Toronto (Ontario) and Del Negro's Francophone Montreal (Québec) in central Canada. To this Canadian profile, American regional identities were added: two southern Californians (Los Angeles for me, San Diego for Verdicchio), and one then-Texan (College Station for Del Negro—who has since returned to Canada (Newfoundland), and teaches at St. John's University). As for our Italian identities: two were Italian-

---

[1] To be fair however, the IASA (Italian American Studies Association) used to be called the AIHA (American Italian Historical Association) and it has always been international, with regular members and participants from Canada and Italy, and occasionally from elsewhere (Australia, Argentina, Great Britain, etc.)—as Laura Ruberto recently reminded me.

born: I was born in Terracina, southern Lazio, Verdicchio in Naples, Campania, and Del Negro is a second-generation Abruzzese-Belgian—and all are part of the post-World War II Italian immigrant cohort, all central-southern Italians, all remain fluent Italian dialect speakers and speakers of standard Italian. Significantly, all three make the question of Italian and Italian diaspora identity the focus of their professional lives (see: infra Contributors.). Between us, we covered a good deal of geographic and cultural ground.

All three members of that diasporic, tri-national, bi-continental panel had actively straddled these divides for decades, and we now agreed to reflect together on how these multiple identities had impacted our personal lives, consciousness, and our scholarly work in university and public spheres. What was unique about *this* triangulation? What cultural and linguistic translations did it entail? (Recall that *trans-latio/translatione*, had, for a millennium, referred to *cultural* translation, not linguistic). How did we strategically self-identify and why? And what sorts of scholarly output had it produced?

In my essay, "Evolving Triangulations within the Canada-Italy-USA Borderlands," I reflect on such questions. From early ethnographic studies on Italian traditional song in Toronto, to ballads in the Appennino Pavese, *neo-tarantismo* in the Salento (Puglia), healers in southern Lazio, and diaspora oral history in California—progressively informed by auto-ethnographic perspectives and sensibilities—I have come to consciously embrace and practice several triangulations, both with respect to scholarly content and modes of representation. As it has evolved from the experience of a first-generation university-educated immigrant of Southern Italian peasant stock in a post-WWII Italian community of Toronto, to the founding of the Italian Oral History Institute in Los Angeles, my scholarly persona presents a paradigm shift that both derives from and straddles traditional academic and public settings, and consciously resists entrenched Italian academic (literary) paradigms. This approach seeks to combine both academic and public sector, both written and oral, in fields of enquiry (i.e., folklore, oral history) which themselves straddle such divides, methodologies, and modes of representation. My essay revisits the how and why of this particular scholarly evolution as an Italian and diaspora oral history and oral culture advocate.

In Giovanna Del Negro's essay: "Never Canadian Enough": Chronic Otherness and Working-Class Cosmopolitanism in the Experience of an Immigrant Academic," she explores growing up in Montreal during heated debates about language and Québecois identity. Outings with her mother often included disapproving looks, and, as she got older, she frequently found herself explaining her name. "Yes, it is Italian, but I was born here." At home, her parents' values were sometimes at odds with her own. It is within this context of chronic otherness and the ethnic politics of Québec that her work on immigrant women, the *passeggiata*, and "Nonna Maria" emerged. As a folklorist living in Texas, her hyphenated identity was seldom recognized, but it profoundly shaped her academic identity. Currently, she has returned to Canada, as a professor of gender studies at St. John's University, Newfoundland.

In "Photographic and Filmic Images of Cultural Triangulation," Pasquale Verdicchio explains how, having lived now for most of his adult life in the United States, longer than he has lived anywhere else, he nevertheless travels to, and continues to maintain close relationships and domicile in Canada and Italy. Living a tripartite life, as it were, the terms by which he negotiates each separate environment tends to hybridize and blend. As a result, he has found visual imagery to be the most apt manner by which such an existence might be represented. In his paper, he discusses the work of photographers and filmmakers who also represent what we might call a triangulated mode of existence and expression. He pays close attention to the work of Toronto photographer Vincenzo Pietropaolo, and Montreal filmmaker Paul Tana as particularly engaged artists whose Canadian reality is itself conditioned by the "extra added."[2]

---

[2] I wish to thank Dean Anthony Julian Tamburri of the John D. Calandra Italian American Institute, for a resident Research Fellowship (Oct 15-Nov 9, 2018) on the theme of "Transnationalism and Identity," which allowed me to focus on this writing and to encourage further development of these linked essays. I also acknowledge my co-fellows and the stimulating discussions on "diaspora" in which we engaged, which further helped fine-tune this essay: Rosemary Serra, Sabrina Vellucci, Roberto Dolci.

Never Canadian Enough
Chronic Otherness and Working-Class Cosmopolitanism in the Experience of an Immigrant Academic

Giovanna P. Del Negro

1. Unmarked Ethnic, Anthropology Lite, and Faux Cosmopolitan

In 2005, I was short-listed for a folklore position that was cross-appointed with Ethnic Studies in an American university. I found out through the grapevine that my application had caused a heated debate about whether my work on Italian immigrant women in Montreal could be called "ethnic studies research." It appears that certain members of the department were under the impression that white European ethnics from Canada didn't fit the bill. For these scholars, ethnic studies was by definition the study of racial others—even though the job ad failed to stipulate that only those working on people of color need apply. As an Italian-Canadian scholar who had admired Robert F. Harney's pioneering research on ethnicity and immigration in Canada (Harney 1974, 1975, 1978, 1979a, 1979b, 1979c, 1980), I found this attitude puzzling and US-centric. But clearly, for some of the faculty in this department, the categories of race or ethnicity were synonymous with African-Americans, Latinxs, or Asians. In the job interview, I acknowledged the crucial role that race plays in American society, but I also emphasized that the categories of race and ethnicity are constructed in differing ways in differing historical periods and social contexts, and that ethnicity itself is a significant social phenomenon worthy of study. Talking with members of the search committee, I was able to prove my "ethnic studies" credentials.[1] After having done, so, however, another obstacle awaited me: within a few minutes of meeting the Dean, I soon realized that she had nothing but contempt for my discipline of folklore studies. Barely concealing her hostility, she snidely asked me to explain the difference between folklore and anthropology, the implication being that folklore was merely a sub-discipline of anthropology, or worse, an antiquated field surpassed by anthropology. Attempting to answer her question, I pointed out the affinity between the two traditions—that like folklorists, many anthropologists are interested in expressive forms like verbal art, vernacular architecture, or outsider art, while folklorists like myself do ethnographic research rooted in participant observation. I also went on to explain the history of folklore and its distinctive contributions—Benjamin Botkin's work with the WPA, the development of the folklife movement in Europe, and the performance studies revolution in 1970s folklore—but my words fell on deaf ears. At the time, I was upset about what had happened, but

---

[1] I had taken ethnic studies courses in my MA and PhD programs, worked closely as a PhD student with a well-known historian of immigration and ethnicity, taught two different courses in the Ethnic Studies Department at Bowling Green State University, where I did my Master's degree, conducted fieldwork and published scholarly research on the Italian community in Montreal, and had just embarked upon new projects on Jewish comedians (2010), the Italian-Polish humor of Judy Tenuta, (2018) and the stand-up comedy of Shazia Mirza, a Muslim comic from the UK. The research in this area also led me to explore the representation of Jewish women in the films of Woody Allen (2014).

with the benefit of hindsight, I realized that the roadblocks I encountered during my job interview were all the more troubling to me because they resonated with the ethnic and cultural politics I experienced growing up as the daughter of Italian immigrants in the complex national and provincial politics of 1970s Québec.

Drawing on autoethnographic methods and writings from folkloristics, anthropology, and ethnic studies, this essay explores my experiences as a folklorist and Canadian ethnic in the American academy, a child and young adult in Quiet Revolution era Québec,[2] fieldworker in Italy, and a scholar in Newfoundland. I examine how the chronic otherness of my youth carried into my workplaces in Texas and Newfoundland, and the way I learned to negotiate shifting power relations and subject positionings as I straddled the geographical, cultural, and temporal boundaries—boundaries among Canada, the US, and post-WWII Italy—on which this volume centers. It would be easy to attribute the anger and frustration that I express throughout this article simply to the various forms of exclusion, discrimination, and elitism I confronted at different stages of my life—never feeling Québécoise

---

[2] The Quiet Revolution was a period in the 1960s marked by secularization, the battle for Francophone language rights, and the rise of a separatist movement which advocated for Québec's independence. The ever-greater threat to public safety by the militant factions of the *Front de Libération du Québec* (the Québec Liberation Front)—which included bombings, kidnappings, and the assassination of the Minister of Labor, Pierre Laporte—finally culminated in the October crises of 1970 and prime minister Pierre Elliott Trudeau's declaration of the War Measures Act, during a time of ostensible peace. The federal government's decision to send soldiers to guard Parliament Hill and patrol the streets of Montreal, where there were curfews and massive arrests without due process, was widely criticized by journalists and politicians alike.

enough, being labelled an outsider in my country of birth, rebuked for my lack of Anglo-Saxon manners, and seeing my Italian immigrant parents, who left the coal mining town of Trazegnies, in Belgium, treated as second-class citizens. In a more profound way, however, my discomfiting rage stems from those systems of gender and ethnic domination that attempt to deny us our agency and keep us silent. By exploring moments from my personal and academic life, I ultimately seek to understand the ways in which issues of identity, cosmopolitanism, and belonging play out in the social situations of intergroup interaction.

In many ways, the situation I confronted on my job interview was baffling. As a folklorist deeply informed by cultural studies and with training in sociology, popular culture, and American studies, I was not in the habit of policing the boundaries of the disciplines within which I operated. To do so, I felt, meant reaffirming outdated, parochial, and romantic visions of my field, which is often represented as the study of static forms of expressive culture that are unable to thrive under the forces of modernity. Indeed, in my early ethnographic work on the *passeggiata* (promenade) and popular culture in Italy (Del Negro 2004), I sought to dispel visions of the Abruzzo as a hotbed of superstition and cultural survivals, and even the bawdy riddles, trickster tales, and lullabies of the Italian immigrant women in Montreal from my first book (Del Negro 2003) were far from quaint, celebratory narratives of the Old World. The child of immigrants, I had parents who were deeply attached to their villages, families back home, and ethnic enclave. At the same time, though, they were open to the new experiences that they encountered in the grocery stores, restaurants, cleaners, and *dépanneurs* (convenience stores) that they owned and that put them in contact with people from a wide range of ethnic and class backgrounds. I, too, felt an affinity toward members of my community, but I also felt drawn to the world of cultural difference that surrounded me. The French-Canadian waitresses with their beehive hairdos who worked at my parents' restaurant were a constant source of fascination for me. I remember being excited when my eldest brother, who had a brief career as a French-language pop singer with the stage name of Danero, would receive social calls from the glamorous France Castel and Claude Blanchard—two well-known Québécois singers. However, I believe that if it weren't for my hyphenated identity, my double-consciousness, my feelings of both belonging and not belonging, and my senses of both attraction and distance to the differing ethnic and class worlds around me, I doubt very much I would have become a folklorist. The chronic otherness I often experienced growing up strongly influenced my interest in folklore and, try as I might to distance myself from all things Italian, I always came back to the place from which I came.

For the Dean that I met at my job interview, however, folklore had little to contribute, and after having been raked over the coals, flustered and seething with anger, I was carted off to give my job talk on the Italian *passeggiata*. In my talk, I described the people of my mother's village of Sasso as working-class cosmopolitans, but in the question-and-answer period that followed, an assistant professor insinuated that the Italians with whom I did fieldwork in the early 1990s were not "true cosmopolitans." In my book on the *passeggiata*, I argue that Sasso's beloved *passeggiata* and Sassani's image of themselves as enlightened cosmopolitans developed in direct response to post-WWII outmigration (and subsequent transmigration) by which fully half of the townsfolk left to go abroad. Responding to what I deemed to be an elitist remark, I said that by Ulf Hannerz, definition Sassani would not qualify as cosmopolitans but that by the standards of Pnini Werbner they would (Hannerz 1990; Werbner 2006). I went on to add that many of the returning émigrés who call Sasso their home speak more than one language and are better travelled than many of the middle-class students I teach, who have never left the state of Texas. As I show in my research, the residents of Sasso are not immune from the influence of modernity. To the contrary, the factories along *la zona industriale* (industrial zone) are owned by foreign multinationals, and the women in the community make clothes for designer labels that are sold in boutiques throughout Europe. The elderly widows in the town, who dressed in traditional black attire, speak both French and Italian, and they watch Argentinian *telenovelas*, and young people listen to Euro pop and world music. Senegalese, Persian, and Algerian peddlers periodically came to Sasso to sell their wares, and many of those who left, as my parents did, returned to visit with their Canadian-born children, who were raised watching the San Remo song festival and enjoyed the music of Celentano, Mina, and Gigliola Cinquetti, right alongside French-Canadian groups like *Harmonium* and *Beau Dommage*. The contemporary Sassani who live away from the centers of power blend old and new in ways that defy provincial visions of modernity or cosmopolitanism. To add insult to injury, one irritated faculty member at my interview told me that Sasso was far from *la piccola Parigi dell'Abruzzo*—a term Sassani half-jokingly and half-seriously used to refer to their town—and that she had seen countless other places in Italy that were much more beautiful. Yes, Sassani know that their town is far from being the City of Lights. But for many in a village that survived the onslaught of massive outmigration, poverty, and economic hardship and was able to rebuild itself, the Sasso of today is as admirable, attractive, and open to the world as any of the other places to which their townsfolk emigrated—Belgium, Australia, Switzerland, France, Germany, Canada, and the United States. Ultimately, the departmental politics of this job search relegated my research to the margins of ethnic studies, and the Italians of my fieldwork, for some at least, were too common, migrant, working-class, and local to be able to claim a term that is generally reserved for wealthy globetrotters. With one dismissive remark, Sassani were labeled "faux cosmopolitans."

At this point in my career I had three authored books under my belt and had just started co-editing the flagship journal of my field, but after this disastrous experience, I felt humiliated. The feelings of exclusion that I sometimes felt growing up came flooding back. Here, however, the bully was not the xenophobe but elitist academics who cannot bring themselves to see meaning and beauty in the Abruzzese dialect or in the *passeggiata*, unless it occurs in Rome or Milan. I was unable to defend the good name of the people of Sasso in the same way that, as a child, I often felt powerless to shield my parents from the disapproving looks they received from passersby because they spoke Italian and Belgian French, ate spaghetti, and dressed in ways that were often viewed as strange and foreign. Growing up, I did not feel underprivileged. My parents had money to pay the rent, feed us, and clothe us, but they felt ashamed about their lack of formal schooling, and I observed firsthand what this kind of social stigma did to their self-confidence and sense of self-worth. Unlike Italian immigration in the US, the waves of migration from Italy to Canada took place mostly after 1945. By the 1970s, there were more than 150,000 immigrant and ethnic Italians living in Montreal, a city of just over 2,500,000 (Ornstein 2007). While the working-class Francophone majority in the city experienced exploitation and humiliation at the hands of the Anglophone elite and could in some ways be welcoming, anti-immigrant bias in Montreal could be intense. After emigrating to Canada, my parents initially found work in the garment industry and eventually experienced upward mobility. But no matter the success that my parents enjoyed—running successful small businesses, becoming homeowners, and seeing their children attend college—my father, especially, had difficulty overcoming his feelings of inadequacy. Born into the peasant class, he lovingly cultivated a vegetable garden in our backyard, which my artisan mother avoided and which helped to salve his injured soul. Ironically, these backyard gardens, which, in the past, had been frowned upon in Montreal as evidence that Italian immigrants were nothing but rubes, today earn high praise by some of the very same people who saw the early Italian immigrants as nothing more than *voleurs de job*—job thieves.

The academic gatekeepers from my job interview found it difficult to believe that the Abuzzese townsfolk or my immigrant parents could be cosmopolitan. Yet, the writings of James Clifford (1992), Ulf Hannerz (2005), and Arjun Appudarai (2011) clearly show cosmopolitanism isn't the domain of elites; to the contrary, it can develop from the bottom up, includes vernacular or working-class forms, and emerges in any multi-centered social world that has an array of influences, people, goods, and worldviews. Indeed, immigrants who feel a deep sense of kinship with their village can feel rooted in multiple locations at the same time, both embracing and rejecting aspects of culture to which they are exposed—by choice, through their work, or because of their offspring. As Richard Werbner observed in his research with the Kalanga people of Botswana, a sense of belonging does not negate openness to cultural difference (2004). In my parent's case, their factory work at Jocardi on Chabanel Street, which made high-end jackets and coats, and the various small businesses they had owned over the years, enabled them to become acquainted with well-known fashion designers, journalists, and politicians. The editor of the Montreal French newspaper, *La Presse*, gave my mother a pin from one of his far away voyages; it was a token of the friendship they had developed over the years, which my mother cherished. After regular hold-ups in the yet to be gentrified St. Lawrence area where my parents had their stores, my parents decided to close up shop. During this period my father worked in a grocery store, and my mother designed, sewed, and altered garments for affluent, middle-aged professional women, whose lives seemed exciting and filled with possibilities. As my brothers and I got older, we pursued differing careers (sales, law, and higher education) in Canada and the USA, and we often brought home a motley crew of friends and colleagues—Francophones, Anglophones of Irish, English and American extraction, along with Persians, Egyptians, Ukrainians, and Greeks. Both of my brothers and I had married outside our ethnic group—a Pakistani, an Afro-Métis Canadian, and a New England Jew—which was uncommon for the period, and my parents, with their limited education, shared meals and animated conversations with Marxist-Leninists, union activists, members of parliament, college professors, librarians, and playwrights. At our weekly Sunday meal, my eldest brother, a serial monogamist, could be expected to show up with one of his many girlfriends, who invariably grew up in a small town outside Montreal. This is how I became familiar with the *habitants* of rural Québec, which I only read about in books like *Kamouraska* (1970) by Anne Hébert. Like many Italian immigrants of the era, my parents interacted with *paesani* (people from their village and near-by towns) and Italians from other regions of Italy, but the Sicilians, Pugliese, and Friulani, whose dialects they didn't share, often seemed as foreign, if not more foreign, than their children's friends. Over the course of years, the apartments in my parents' fiveplex and triplex, across the street from where we lived in the neighborhood of St. Michel, were rented to Italian-Canadians, French-Canadians, Chileans, Moroccans, Rwandans, and Colombians--people from all walks of life: students, teachers, engineers, graphic artists, clerks, office workers, retirees, the unemployed, and welfare recipients.

My parent's hospitality and openness toward the world, however, co-existed alongside their disdain for French-Canadian food and their (perceived) liberal attitudes toward sex, as well as a barely concealed racism toward the recent influx of Haitians and Muslims who had moved into the neighborhood. Despite their racist attitudes, my parents finally accepted my Afro-Métis sister-in-law into our household, but my mother was not too thrilled to hear that my husband and I were going to adopt two older African American girls from the foster care system. In this, they were no more racist than some of my middle-class American relations from my husband's family, who lamented the "lack of hygiene" of the Mexicans they encountered on trips abroad and complained of Italians' "refusal" to speak English in Italy. It is worth noting that the Senegalese immigrants in Sasso had similar experiences as my immigrant parents. They experienced marginalization by the majority native population and, at the same time, scoffed at the lack of cultural refinement of the Italians who haggled with them in the public square where they sold their crafts. If these examples show anything, it is that cosmopolitanism by itself doesn't necessarily translate into a greater good. On the contrary, it often involves what Mamadou Diouf maintains are "rites of social exclusiveness [which seek to] maintain a homogenized culture that excludes foreign values." (Diouf 2000, 694)

2. CFA: Come from Away

In 1997, I accepted a position as an assistant professor in the Folklore Department at Memorial University in St. John's, Newfoundland, Canada. Even though my decision to accept the job was bittersweet, as I was leaving my husband behind, I was looking forward to going back home. At the job interview, I remember having two intensely Canadian moments. On my tour of the island, while stopping for a break at a small convenience store, I discovered my favorite childhood treat. As I picked up my May West, a white moon cake filled with vanilla creme center and covered in dark chocolate, I was taken back to my primary school days in Montreal. I remembered my parents' grocery store on Belanger and 9th Avenue, our second-floor apartment right above, the private courtyard with easy access to my aunt and uncle's place, and the fire exit doors of the *7ème art* theater, which I used to sneak into French dubbed American movies. Everything we needed was nearby—the homes of our cousins, which were within walking distance, the Cousineau bakery, with its delicious French bread and Belgian rice pies, the family-owned Favreau drug store, with its French-Canadian pharmacists, who were always friendly and eager to help, and one of the best record stores in the city. Farther away, on Jean Talon Street, we had *Conca d'oro* (Golden Vessel), an Italian deli and pastry shop, *La Consolata* (Our Lady of Consolation) church, banks with Italian-speaking personnel, and the *Patronato Italo-Canadese per l'Assistenza agli Immigrati* (the Italian-Canadian Charitable Organization for Immigrants), an association that provided assistance to Italian immigrants, including Saturday morning language classes for families who wanted their children to learn standard Italian. All these places continue to exist today, but now they largely cater to a more ethnically diverse clientele of Haitians, Algerians, and Vietnamese, who have moved into the area and established their own businesses and places of worship. With its formal and informal institutions and organization, including Italian language newspapers, radio stations, and Sunday TV broadcasts, our neighborhood displayed what Raymond Breton referred to as a high degree of institutional completeness (Breton 1964: 193). Nevertheless, St. Michel was still a predominantly Francophone borough, and as such, it had well established shopping arcades, bars, clubs, grocery stores, parks, and hospitals, which had been serving its Québécois residents for many years. A historically low-income and working-class neighborhood, St. Michel had its fair share of restaurants, which featured Québécois food and snacks such as steamed hot dogs, *poutine* (French fries with cheese curds and gravy), and *paté chinois* (shepard's pie). And it had Anglophone institutions as well. I attended St. Finbar Elementary and John F. Kennedy High, English-language schools named after Irish-Catholic figures, which reflected the religious beliefs of both the Irish and the French in Canada.

The second most intensely Canadian moment I experienced during my job interview at Memorial University occurred when my folklore colleague, Peter Narváez, turned the dial of his car radio to the CBC station (Canadian Broadcasting Corporation), while he was giving me a tour of the Avalon Peninsula.[3] I had always enjoyed the CBC's person-on-the-street report-

---

[3] The CBC is a beloved cultural institution in Canada, and this was not lost on Korean-Canadian actress Sandra Oh, who in a recent appearance on *Saturday Night Live* showed her Canadian pride by wearing a T-shirt with the CBC logo on it.

ing and the show *As it Happens*, with well-known Canadian personalities and Francophone politicians, who sounded like they were from Shawinigan. I even got schmaltzy watching Tim Hortons' commercials (coffee and donut shop) on television on cold, snowy nights in my house on Pennywell Road, which was right across the street from the home of Mary Walsh, a cast member of the well-known, Newfoundland-based comedy show, *This Hour Has Twenty-Two Minutes*. When I arrived in St. John's, I finally thought, "I am home," but I soon experienced new ways of being marginalized in the country of my birth. In Québec, I was always a hyphenated ethnic, not Canadian and not *une Québécoise de pure laine* (a dyed in the wool Quebecker). Doing fieldwork in Italy, the residents of my mother's home town saw me as *l'Americana* (from North America), a "Fangarilli" (my mother's clan name) by birth, who spoke an antiquated dialect, but not fully Italian.[4] In Newfoundland, I was what the locals called a CFA (Come from Away). Newfoundland joined confederation in

---

[4] Folklorist Kimberly Lau observes similar dynamics in a 2002 autoethnographic account. As the daughter of a Japanese-Hawaiian mother and Chinese American father, Lau's relationship to her Asian identity has never been simple. Indeed, her essay aptly reveals how her sense of self and other's perception of her varied greatly depending on context and region, as well as her own feelings of ethnic insecurity. At an Asian American Studies conference she attended to scout for prospective job candidates for her department, Lau felt uncomfortable and out of place. Not only did she feel she was not Asian enough, by comparison to all of the other participants at the meeting, but she was not the Asian Americanist that everyone assumed her to be. She felt doubly displaced—culturally and disciplinarily. In the East Coast, Lau's Southern Californian inflected speech (i.e., "Valley Girl" accent) sometimes made people chuckle, but in many ways, she could be her own worst critic, trying to appease her doubts about whether she could legitimately lay claim to her Asian identity by taking Chinese classes, which, as it turned out, proved to be disastrous, because she was tone deaf.

1949, and in the 1990s Canadians were still seen as outsiders in the province. In this context, I was positioned as Canadian, not Italian-Canadian, and the residual pre-Confederation identity of Newfoundland made being "Canadian," an Other, a person with whom one did not share a nationality. Even though Québec is culturally and geographically closer to Newfoundland than it is to Ohio, Indiana, or Texas, and though I didn't hail from the sometimes-reviled Anglo-Saxon bastion of power and privilege (Toronto), I still came from the mainland. From a Central Italian perspective, however, Newfoundland and the Abruzzo share a great deal in common: they both have been historically underdeveloped, and both have only recently freed themselves from economic dependence on their capital cities (Ottawa and Rome).

My journey back to Canada was by no means simple and included many pit-stops along the way—graduate school in the Midwest, a Jewish-Italian wedding in Montreal, over one year of fieldwork in Italy, and a move to Texas shortly before departing for Newfoundland. While Newfoundland only had a small French-speaking population, it had an even smaller Italian community. As it turned out, life in Newfoundland was, in some ways, more familiar than I had expected. Like Montreal, St. John's is rich with music and theater, and has a well-established art scene, and like Québec, Newfoundland has a separatist movement. In terms of the particulars of my cultural heritage, I was ethnically distant from the majority of Newfoundlanders, who were largely of Irish and English descent. However, in a more abstract, though nonetheless palpable way, I was in my "home and native land," and the quintessential byproduct of the 1970s multiculturalism of the Pierre Elliott Trudeau years, which promoted the idea of Canada as a cultural mosaic, a place where immigrants could acculturate to their new society without having to lose their linguistic and ethnic identity.

3. SETTLEMENT PATTERNS AND ETHNIC INVISIBILITY

My parents and brothers moved to ever bigger places as they left their small village in the Abruzzo for a mining town in Belgium and the garment district of Montreal. In contrast, I left the hustle and bustle of the city for small college towns in the American Midwest and eventually spent many years in College Station, the home of Texas A&M University. I spent the first two years away from Montreal working toward my M.A. in popular culture at Bowling Green State University in Bowling Green, Ohio, with a longer stint at Indiana University in Bloomington doing my Ph.D. in folklore and American studies. The home of Alfred Kinsey, Bloomington is a small town with a rich cultural life of repertoire films, bohemian coffeehouses, and ethnic restaurants. College Station, though significantly larger in population than Bowling Green or Bloomington, felt smaller and more insular. As a native Montrealer, my inability to walk or take the bus to work was difficult enough, but the stultifying heat of central Texas, with its suburban architecture and lack of public culture, left me at odds with my environment. Like many of my colleagues, who attended graduate school on the East Coast or places like California, with its temperate climate, I was a fish out of water.

The sense of alienation, however, also extended to my place of work and the progressive erasure of my ethnic difference in a town that favored cultural conformity above all else. Not only was I a "partner placement" hire in a department that had historically been unfriendly to folklorists, I was an ethnographer, a scholar who challenged established literary methods of research. While I felt socially, culturally, and disciplinarily displaced, my ethnicity, which had constantly been at the foreground of my experience in Montreal, both positively and negatively, was now relegated to the background. The die-hard Aggies that I taught at Texas A&M fiercely celebrated their "normalcy" in opposition to their rivals from the University of Texas at Austin, who were considered "weird." Therefore, it was no surprise that second- or third-generation Czech, German, and Mexican students in my courses seldom talked about their ethnicity. They were first and foremost Americans. Similarly, in most of my interactions with people in my neighborhood or storekeepers, I was just another Yankee, an academic transplant who spoke English and had an unusual family name. As an international student in the US, I had been considered Canadian, but in Texas, both my nationality and cultural background were left unacknowledged. Overnight, I became an invisible ethnic without an enclave or like-minded intellectual community to call my own.

My sense of dislocation, however, began even before I had my job interview in Texas. Approaching an older, established faculty member at A&M about how to seek a partner placement position, I was told to make my CV look more like that of an English scholar. My work experience with *Centro Donne* (a non-profit

Italian immigrant women's association in Montreal), *Federazione Italiana Lavoratori Emigrati e Famiglie* (a group that organized community events and provided services to Italians living abroad), CIBL105 (a Francophone radio station, where I played Italian popular music), French and English language newspapers and theater, and public sector folklore organizations in Canada and the US—all had to be erased. We all have to frame our backgrounds to appeal to prospective employer, especially those of us who work in underrepresented disciplines. What rankled me, however, is that both my community experience and ethnographic fieldwork had to be downgraded in order to appear respectable. I got the distinct impression that this period in my life had to be represented as a brief detour on my way to becoming the academic that I am today. Nothing, of course, could be farther from the truth. The on-the-ground activism of my early years has not only shaped who I am as person, it is at the core of what I do in my chosen profession as a folklorist. Not everyone in the department would have been offended by my quirky CV, but as a junior scholar coming up through the ranks, I couldn't help but feel anger, resentment, and a deep sense of loss at having to excise these parts of my identity. My degree in popular culture did not make matters any easier for me, as traditional visions of English literature are set against the study of commercially driven forms of mass entertainment, which even today are often viewed as crass and devoid of aesthetic merit.

The irony is that while faculty members in the English department published on the rise of middlebrow book clubs, popular television shows, and movies, I was criticized by a colleague for not teaching Mark

Twain in a course I developed on women's stand-up comedy. I'm convinced that if I had been teaching the canon or if I had been a man, he might not have felt so comfortable about telling me what to include in my syllabus. My course ended up drawing heavily on performance-oriented work, feminist writings on humor, and cultural studies, and I required my students to perform a five-minute stand-up comedy routine. Likewise, when I taught the first "Introduction to Cultural Studies" course in the department, a graduate student reported that one of my colleagues told him that my course didn't truly qualify as "cultural studies." My Birmingham school inflected class, with readings by Gramsci, Williams, Marx, Adorno, Marcuse, Hall, McRobbie, and Mercer was simply too sociological and ethnographic for this particular critic. When I approached this colleague and suggested that, coming from different disciplinary backgrounds, she and I might view the interdisciplinary field of cultural studies in different ways, she politely acquiesced, but it was quite clear that she didn't feel that my perspective was legitimate. Early in my teaching career, I vowed to draw extensively on my training, even if it raised eyebrows, and from the outset, I would not, nor could I, even if I tried, make myself into a mainstream English scholar. I also knew that deciding to pursue a new project in the area of women's stand-up comedy was inevitably going to elicit the disapproval of certain factions in the English Department and that I could also have problems receiving funding for my research from the university. Ultimately, academic freedom allowed me to push back, but it didn't always endear me to my less open-minded colleagues.

But if my broadly interdisciplinary training in sociology, folklore, and popular culture was out of place, so was my ethnicity. In Montreal, I was unavoidably ethnic. Most of the time in the US, my ethnicity disappeared. I was just "white," and if my Italian heritage was recognized at all, it was thought of as almost ornamental. At other moments, though, it came roaring to the foreground. When I went up for my third-year review at Texas A&M, there was a new Dean who was keen on flexing his muscles, and I unexpectedly ended up in the crosshairs of his new administration. Hearing that the College's vote on my case was evenly split, I felt defeated. It seemed that everything I worked so hard to accomplish was flushed down the drain because of the fear-mongering tactics of a new regime, which felt perfectly empowered to change the rules midstream. Evidently, lazy academics like us needed to be given greater incentives to make sure that we worked harder. I consulted with a very senior colleague about the College's review. He did not know quite what to make of this decision, but he reassured me that if my publications were physically in print before tenure, and if I demonstrated that I had a new research project underway, that I should be fine. Thus, in addition to having a book manuscript that had received positive readers' reports and was accepted for publication by a well-respected academic press, a co-authored book that was under review at a second well-respected academic press, articles in the flagship journal of my discipline, and special issues either accepted or appearing in print, I had to show that I had started a completely new research project that would translate into post-tenure publications.

In hindsight, my senior colleague gave me good advice by telling me not to put too much stock in this assessment, but he made it clear that he did not approve of my unvarnished disgust for the Dean's Advisory Committee (faculty members who make recommendations to the dean) and the upper administration. It seems that I was poorly schooled in genteel, Anglo-Saxon manners, as I failed to show the proper deference toward a system that was supposed to reward those who work hard. Being told not to be too "hot-headed" about the situation in which I found myself by a male scholar whose whiteness and propriety were unimpeachable, it became abundantly clear that I would never truly become a full-fledged member of the club. If I let my "hot-headedness" get the better of me, I could, at any moment, run the risk of being too ethnic, and in so doing, jeopardize my membership in the society of professors who take pride in living by the principles of cool rationality. Today's neoliberal university is top-heavy with administrators and fixated on ever more complex schemes of metrics and standards for measuring scholarly productivity.

The decisions that are made by university bureaucracies, however, occur within a larger context of departmental and disciplinary politics and changing administrations, which constantly rethink the means by which faculty are assessed, as if rigid systems of metrics alone can decide the fate of tenure-track and tenured professors. We are made to believe the metrics and standards exist to treat everyone equally. But standards must always be interpreted, and complex metrics can be used to reinforce bias, as well as undermine it. I heeded the warnings of the new regime; I worked long hours to make sure that all of my publications came out before tenure, and, fortunately for me, my tenure case went smoothly. When my time came, I passed with flying colors, but I fretted anxiously throughout the whole process, like most junior scholars, because I knew that the process of achieving tenure and the merit structure on which that process is based are flawed. Throughout my career, I have seen promising young academics turned down for tenure, and candidates with weak records promoted because it was the politically expedient thing to do. The English Department at Texas A&M is made up of many talented, hardworking faculty who received the recognition they deserve, but for those of us who exist in marginalized disciplines and inherit pre-existing histories that are not of our own making, the road ahead, at least from my perspective, was rockier than most.

My experiences of ethnic marginalization and the marginalization I experienced as a scholar of populist aesthetics from a discipline pushed to the periphery of the academy have resonated with one another in complex ways. While all individuals experience multi-dimensional identity, the sense of marginalization is heightened for immigrants and ethnics who live at the meeting place between cultures and have to negotiate differential identity[5] on a daily basis.[6] In the US, where

---

[6] Historically, folklore had been defined as the exclusive domain of tightly knit, homogeneous communities bound together by a shared culture. Richard Bauman's work on differential identity (1971) instead shows that folklore can indeed flourish in situations in which people may not necessarily have a single common culture. Bauman argues that expressive culture can only be fully understood by taking into account the richly complex social base from which it develops. In this reconceptualization of the field, it not only becomes possible to study the interactions among disparate groups that come into contact with one another, but it also becomes possible to analyze the process by which those differences could

questions of race hold a distinctive centrality, visibility is the hub around which identity politics turns, and the central issue for many European ethnics is the choice between assimilation or what Herbert J. Gans called "symbolic ethnicity" (Gans 1979). In the Québec of the 1970s, the paramount marker of identity was language, and the language-based ethnic politics of the period helped suggest a very different social dynamic. At that time, many European immigrants and ethnics *could* pass, as long as they kept their mouths shut, both literally and figuratively, and everyday life involved an odd pattern in which one would rocket back and forth between invisibility and hyper-visibility. Moving between Canadian and American contexts, and also when shifting from the field of folklore studies to the wider disciplinary space of English, I experience something similar: my identity as other—Canadian, first-generation Italian ethnic, folklorist—is invisible as long as I don't draw attention to who I am. Flying under the radar has its advantages, but it can be disempowering as well, leaving one with the feeling of being disingenuous if one doesn't speak out and vulnerable if one does. In Québec, before the Quiet Revolution, Francophones were chastised by entitled Anglophones for not "speaking white," a phenomenon that poet Michèle Lalonde famously explored in her 1968 poem of that name, where she took the slur as an emblem of all manner of power relations expressed through language. While post-WWII Italian immigrants who lived in Montreal frequently learned French as their second

---

be exchanged and assimilated in contexts of situated action and performance.

language, they were savvy enough to know that English was the language of money, and the majority of Italians during this period sent their children to English schools. We, too, learned to speak white, not dago, and not to attract the attention or the ire of those in power. These days, I find myself more at home with a postcolonial scholar from the Caribbean and a South Asian economist who grew up in Rome—people whose sense of displaced identity and ethnic solidarity resonate with my own. Trying to navigate a foreign domain and make common cause with other immigrants, my experience is not so different from that of my parents—though, working in the insular world of the academy, I do not experience the cross-class interactions to the extent that they did.

Of course, folklorists don't experience the intense discrimination that ethnic minorities or linguistically marginalized groups do, but there is no question that we are far from the corridors of power in the academy. It is no accident that I am committed to folklore's populist vision of culture, and I can't help but feel that this commitment is tied to a historical period in which my sense of self was formed, the moment of Québec history in which Italian immigrant culture was frequently devalued or misunderstood. Where some of my Anglophone friends in Québec saw nothing but kitsch and bad taste in my parent's ceramic floors, marble-covered front porch, plastic-covered sofas, and handmade garden ornaments, I saw meaning, beauty, creativity, and defiance in the face of a society that could often be hostile. Therefore, to discover a field premised on the study of the expressive culture of marginalized groups was a liberating experience, and working out the implications of a populist aesthetic has been at the heart of my scholarly project.

The issue of populism and culture brings us back to the vignette that opened this essay—the conflict over who might be considered cosmopolitan. I did not go into the field seeking working-class cosmopolitans, but for the people of Sasso, this was an essential feature of their town's social life. Only a scholar predisposed to elitist visions of cultural diversity would miss this facet of Sassani society or dismiss it as insignificant. The professional classes say that they prize travel and formal education because they expose the person to other ways of seeing the world and provide a wider view of humanity. "Travel broadens the mind," or so the saying goes. Having an expansive view of social life is certainly desirable, but by denying the ways in which travel and education are tied to class privilege, the traditional view of cosmopolitanism often devolves into nothing more than bourgeois ideology, a card to play in a game of social status. Here, I find it ironic that the self-styled arbiters of cosmopolitanism were the most provincial —completely unwilling to admit that the residents of a small town in central Italy could be anything other than rubes. I still believe that having a broad, cross-cultural view of the universe is desirable. But my experience with the American job for which I interviewed—no less than my experience as an ethnic in Québec, a Canadian in Texas, or a CFA in Newfoundland—showed me that our respect for cultural difference can never be taken alone. It always emerges in particular social situations, is always tied to and develops its meaning in the context of particular material conditions, intergroup politics, dynamics of visibility or audibility, and status hierarchies, and our sense of self is profoundly shaped by those forces. And it is because of this that our work as scholars of Italy and the Italian diaspora is so essential. Following the adventures of Italian identity as it wends its way through historical conditions of the Mediterranean and, eventually, the world, we develop a unique perspective on the politics of culture. In this sense, perhaps the doing of Italian studies and folklore studies is a project of a deeper cosmopolitanism, one that knows where it came from and sees where it is going.

Works Cited

Appadurai, Arjun. 2011. "Cosmopolitanism from Below: Some Ethical Lessons from The Slums of Mumbai." *The Salon.* 4: 32-43.

Bauman, Richard. 1971. "Differential Identity and the Social Base of Folklore." *Journal of American Folklore* 84 (331): 31-41.

Berger, M. Harris and Giovanna P. Del Negro 2004. *Identity and Everyday Life: Essays in the Study of Folklore, Music, and Popular Culture.* Music/Culture Book Series. Middletown, CT: Wesleyan University Press.

Breton, Raymond. 1964. "Institutional Completeness of Ethnic Communities and the Personal Relations of Immigrants." *American Journal of Sociology* 70 (2): 193-205.

Clifford, James. 1992. "Travelling Cultures." In *Cultural Studies*, edited by Lawrence Grossberg, Cary Nelson, and Paula A. Treichler 96-116. New York: Routledge

Del Negro, Giovanna P. 2018. "Petit Flower, Giver Goddess, and Duchess of Discipline: Sexual Non-Conformity, Play, and Camp Humor in the Performance of Judy Tenuta. In *Gender and Humor: Interdisciplinary and International Perspectives*, edited by Delia Chiaro and Raffaella Baccolini, 288-297. Routledge Research in Cultural and Media Studies. New York: Routledge.

———. 2014. "Woody's Women: Jewish Domesticity and the Unredeemed Ghost of Hanukkah to Come." In *Woody on Rye: Jewishness in the Films and Plays of Woody Allen*, edited by Vincent Brook and Marat Grinberg, 143-170. Waltham, MA: Brandeis University Press.

———. 2010. "The Bad Girls of Jewish Comedy: Gender, Ethnicity, and Whiteness in Post WWII America." In *A Feminine Mystique? Jewish Women in Post War America*, edited by Hasia R. Diner, Shira Kohn, and Rachel Kranson, 144-159. New Brunswick, NJ: Rutgers University Press.

———. 2004. *The Passeggiata and Popular Culture in an Italian Town: Folklore and the Performance of Modernity*. Montreal: McGill-Queen's University Press.

———. 2003 (1997). *Looking Through My Mother's Eyes: Life Stories of Nine Italian Immigrant Women in Canada*. Second Edition. Montreal: Guernica Press.

Diouf, Mamadou. 2000. "The Senegalese Murid Trade Diaspora and the Making of a Vernacular Cosmopolitanism." *Public Culture* 12 (3): 679-702.

Gans, Herbert J. 1979. "Symbolic Ethnicity: The Future of Ethnic Groups and Cultures in America." *Ethnic and Racial Studies* 2 (1):1-20.

Hannerz, Ulf. 2005. "Two Faces of Cosmopolitanism." *Statsvetenskaplig Tidskrift* 107 (3): 199-213.

———. 1990. "Cosmopolitans and Locals in World Culture." *Theory, Culture, and Society* 7: 237-251.

Harney, Robert. 1980. "The Padrone System and Sojourners in the Canadian North, 1885-1920." In *Pane e Lavoro: The Italian-American Working Class*, edited by George E. Pozzetta, 119-137. Toronto, Ontario.

_____. 1979a. "Men Without Women: Italian Migrants in Canada, 1885-1930." *Canadian Ethnic Studies* 11(1): 29-47.

_____. 1979b. "Montreal's King of Italian Labour: A Case Study of Padronism." *Labour/Le Travailleur* 4(2): 57-84.

_____. 1979c. "The Italian Community in Toronto." In *Two Nations: Many Cultures*, edited by Jean Leonard Elliott, 220-236. Toronto, Ontario: Prentice-Hall.

_____. 1978. "Boarding and Belonging." *Urban History Review* 78 (2): 8-37.

_____. 1977. "The Commerce of Migration." *Canadian Ethnic Studies* (9): 42-53.

_____. 1974. "The Padrone and the Immigrant." *Canadian Review of American Studies* 5 (2): 101-11.

Hébert, Anne. 1970. *Kamouraska*. Paris. Editions du Seuil.

Lalonde, Michèle. 1967. "Speak White." *Terre des hommes: poème pour deux récitants*. Montreal: Éditions du Jour.

Lau, Kimberly J. 2002. "The Text which Is Not One: Dialectics of Self and Culture in Experimental Autoethnography." *Journal of Folklore Research* 39 (2/3): 243-359.

Ornstein, Michael. 1987. "Ethno-Racial Groups in Montreal and Vancouver, 1971-2001: Demographic and Socio-Economic Profile." *Institute for Social Research*. 1-28. Toronto: York University.

Werbner, Richard. 2004. "Cosmopolitan Ethnicity, Entrepreneurship, and the Nation." In *Reasonable Radicals and Citizenship in Botswana: The Public Anthropology of Kalanga Elites*, 63-85. Bloomington: Indiana University Press.

Werbner, Pnini. 2006. "Vernacular Cosmopolitanism." *Anthropology News* 47 (5): 7-11.

Photographic and Filmic Images of Cultural Triangulation

Pasquale Verdicchio

A little over twenty years ago I published a collection of essays entitled *Devils in Paradise*, in which I introduced the term *post-emigrant* as a way to define what I thought might be the end of a specific period in Italian North American writing and the initiation of another (Verdicchio 1996). One of the two epigraphs that open the book cites Sardinian, Antonio Gramsci:

> The starting point of critical elaboration is the consciousness of what one really is and knowing one's self as a product of the historical process to date, which has deposited in you an infinity of traces without leaving an inventory. Therefore, it is imperative at the outset to compile such an inventory (Gramsci 1975, 2, 1363).

At that time I did not explicate the reasons for its use since it seemed both self-explanatory and was meant to be a generative matrix to be further elaborated in a then not too distant future. The phase I envisioned was one that would follow the stories of emigration, immigration and adaptation—those that had been recounted over the span of the preceding decades. Such stories surveyed the landscape of familial histories and staked the ground upon which inhabitation might grow and flourish. It was, in my view, a phase entirely in tune with the Gramsci citation.

His suggestion emerged out of a specific socio-cultural situation that, while not immediately applicable to the case of Italian North America, was nonetheless part of a context inclusive of workers and peasants within the Italian nation and of the Southern question, both of which in turn gave rise (at least in part) to the question of emigration. It is a valuable connection that, despite its apparent specificity, could also be applicable to the experience of ethnic or so-called "minority groups" within a variety of national contexts. Since Italian emigration resulted from the incapacities of the nation to allow citizens the means of survival, the importance of compiling such an inventory cannot be overstated. Yet, were such an inventory reduced to a mere unproblematized list of traits, characteristics, regrets, complaints and accusations, or used in an uncritical way, it would lose its pliability, its ability to evolve, and would likely sink into banality. More importantly, even while emigration and the eventual assimilation into other national spheres and cultures might lead one to predict a truncation of relations, narratives and historical discontinuity, Gramsci's proposal offers an opportunity for regenerative self-assessment.

And so, the term "post-emigrant" sought to identify a border of sorts, across which we might catch glimpses of our own participatory construction of its parameters, which we might identify firsthand, and in short, we assume that most of our cultural production no longer issues from the first generation, but rather from a generationally diverse group of writers, artists, and intellectuals. But indeed, an exciting prospect, in my view, has largely yet to be fully or innovatively enacted.

The use of the term "triangulation" which the initial generative concept for the essays in this collection, dovetails quite nicely with the concept of the post-emigrant approach I have delineated above. What is triangulation? What do we mean by it? What is its purpose, and how is it structured? These are the questions I will attempt to address in the next few pages, illustrating some of these issues through the works of two first-generation individuals who have made triangulation their life's work. I also note that I too am a member of this triangulatory creative group.

How can we begin to conceive of the difference between story and narration? The first elucidates what is assumed to be a reality, while the second becomes a process of continuous discovery. In his book *Storie comuni*, Paolo Jedlowski identifies in the figure of the *witness* the one who facilitates elaboration, someone without whom there would be no historical record (Jedlowski 2000:174-175). How do the stories and traditions of old function in a new context? Too often we tell the stories but fail to propose a narrative or, in other words, establish an historical present of Italian North America.

To illustrate this, I will use a personal anecdote. During one of my parents' visits from Vancouver to San Diego (a triangulation of sorts superimposed upon our first emigration from Naples to Vancouver, and my second to San Diego, where I work, which continues to test the coordinates of a rhizomatic migration still decades later), my three year-old daughter picked up a persistent hiccup. My father, took her into his lap and broke into a rhyme I had not heard him recite before:

> singhiuzz singhiuzz
> vola int' 'o puzz
> nn' 'o dicere a nisciun
> vola 'ncopp' 'a luna
> vola a mar
> va add'a cummar
> vire che te rice
> e vienemmell' 'a dicere.[1]

> Hiccup hiccup
> Fly into the well
> And no one do tell
> Fly up to the moon
> Fly to the sea
> Go to the godmother
> See what she says
> And bring it back to me.

The magical incantation of those words was of course lost to my daughter since they were in *napoletano* (Neapolitan dialect). Their real magic was of course carried by the rhythm rather than the content, a diversion of sorts, working to make those words effective miles, cultures and a generation apart from their source. This may appear as a bit of a tangent, but it is not unrelated to my focus on the work of the two individuals here presented and whom I consider to be among our more creative and important public intellectuals: the photographer, Vincenzo Pietropaolo, and the filmmaker, Paul Tana.

---

[1] Neapolitan nursery rhyme. Personal communication.

I trust that my definition of these two artists as public intellectuals makes obvious the fact that the categories of photographer and filmmaker are too restrictive to fully describe their activities. As a way of briefly presenting them, I will say that their works are wide-ranging, expansive, always incisive in their impact, to initiate dialogue and suggestive narrative strategies.

Tana and Pietropaolo do not merely tell their stories. They tell us their stories via the stories of others, through multiple points of view, in all their glories, failures, pain, and marginalizations. Rather than a normative Italian experience they elaborate a diversity that compels the viewer to extend their own perspective toward a comparative cultural approach. After all, cultures are relative, not absolute systems in both their evolution and expression; both these artists are fully involved in illustrating and visually enabling these diverse voices.

Paul Tana's film, *Ricordati di noi*, recounts the rediscovery of film footage from *Teledomenica,* Montreal's first Italian-language television program. Broadcast every Sunday from 1964 to 1994, its highlight was the broadcasting of recorded greetings from relatives and friends in Italy, played to the immigrant community in Québec. Years after its last broadcast, host Giovanni Gargiulo contacted Paul Tana with the news that film reels of the program had been found. With this trove in hand, Tana and a crew of film technicians from the Cinématique Québecoise began their work of collating and restoring this precious record of the life of Montreal's Italian community.

There was, however, one small problem: the films were initially found without their soundtrack. Even after it eventually found, the soundtrack needed to be synched with existing visuals, without any indication of placement. With the assistance of non-hearing Anna Valenziano, who was able to lip-read her way through the film, Tana and his team were finally able to synch the two media. In such a way, the process itself became a sort of triangulation by which vintage images recuperated as faded memories that had fallen out sight, and out of synch with their sound and place in history, were once again restored to clarity and significance.

Vincenzo Pietropaolo's book, *Harvest Pilgrims*, documents the lives of migrant workers in Canada. Besides Pietropaolo's own account of the situation and the photographs, the book contains an imaginary letter from the photographer to one of his subjects. Most likely an amalgam of various laborers he came to know over the years, Pietropaolo addresses the letter to Fermin, who has returned to his native Mexico, following yet another harvest season in Canada. The letter is an attempt to draw closer to those workers through the intimate medium of letter-writing. The photographs in the book are obviously the work of someone who values proximity to his subjects, and not merely of a photographer "shooting" photos for a project. They show a sensitive approach, a caring gaze, rather than an objectifying and detached one.

While one might tend to interpret the letter as an attempt to balance or enhance the photographs, as captions often seem to want to stress what the image supposedly was not completely able to represent, Pietropaolo's letter is itself a candid illustration of the photographer's concerns. It is perhaps not a stretch of the imagination to suggest that Pietropaolo's photographic relationships may stem from his longtime interest in the laboring bodies of the Italians of Toronto, in the displaced culture of his own community. Through that experience, Pietropaolo is able to draw close to the similarity of experiences of other migrants and Italian immigrants. And, perhaps the letter serves as a testimony of those differently-situated correspondences and floating cultural coordinates. With the words "But you are also a worker […] you grow our food," Pietropaolo goes further in recognizing a multiplicity of narratives that, again, do not simply comment on the photographs but make apparent an existential and essential connection: *You are a laborer like other laborers and we all depend on our reciprocal labor in order to survive* (Pietropaolo 2009: 25).

The title *Harvest Pilgrims* suggests yet another dimension of migration. Whether temporary or permanent, migration entails a sense of movement, a hope of return, a sense of multiple connections. *Pilgrims* carries an unspoken assumption of devotional return to a significant and defining place. We might describe as "pilgrimage" even our relationship to favorite recipes, photographs, or meaningful cultural objects and practices. Hence, the citation of my father's rhyme: it too functioned as a pilgrim's touchstone and, like Pietropaolo's letter, as an expression of triangulations that speak to their, and our transitions, and movements between lands, cultures, languages and social roles.

Ricordati di noi illustrates such a pilgrimage in yet another way. Back in the 1960s, Alfredo Gagliardi's program *Teledomenica* made it its task to create a connection between the two realities of Montreal's Italian community, their new home, and the places those immigrants had left behind. Realities that, with the passing of time, were becoming more and more distant from each other. Functioning both as pilgrimage and testimonial, the back and forth messages communicated via television were an attempt to keep relationships alive. After the program ended, the communal exchanges withered away and the materials that served as witness to that evolving narrative were dispersed, separated and, in an ironic illustration of the realities of migration, lost their voices/languages and were literally muted. Tana's recovery of the narrative was in a most meaningful way, part of a communal effort and, as such, re-established through the documentation of the process, the witnessing of it as a central element of the story/narrative.

Both these public intellectuals, Tana and Pietropaolo, move within an ever-expanding public sphere in which the points of triangulation must remain movable as they are also situated within specific cultural contexts. Using the coordinates of their own cultures (already at work negotiating space within two dominant and distinct cultural contexts in Canada—one Anglophone Toronto and Montreal) Tana and Pietropaolo extend themselves to generate a renewed cultural imaginary and network vis-à-vis the hegemonic cultures of their places of residence, as well as with respect to the normative parameters of *italianità* (Italianness).

Finally, for the interactive processes that both Pietropaolo and Tana enable, their triangulations include a temporal dimension in the orientation of the present. They represent a process of historicization that makes their works not merely expressions of a singular artistic vision but that of a collective re-membering or re-collection of experiences, moments, associations and, of course, in this case, not only dispersed materials but also dispersed identities and relationships.

Works Cited

Gramsci 1975. Antonio Gramsci, *Quaderni del carcere*. Valentino Gerratana, ed. Torino: Einaudi, 2:1363.

Jedlowski 2000. Paolo Jedlowski. *Storie comuni: La narrazione nella vita quotidiana. Testi e pretesti*. Milano: Bruno Mondadori.

Pietropaolo 2009. Vincenzo Pietropaolo. *Harvest Pilgrims*. Toronto: Between the Lines.

Tana 2007. Paul Tana. *Ricordati di noi!/Souviens-toi de nous!* Montréal: Locomotion. DVD.

Verdicchio 1996. Pasquale Verdicchio. *Devils in Paradise: Writings on Post-emigrant Cultures*. Toronto: Guernica.

Mexican peach picker. Beamsville, Ontario, Canada, 1986 ©Vincenzo Pietropaolo

Reginald Cabey, from Montserrat, loading cauliflower. Waterford, Ontario, Canada. 1987. ©Vincenzo Pietropaolo

Pasquale Verdicchio • "Photographic and Filmic Images"

Deffina Valle Guitiérrez thinning the apple crop –removing imperfect or excessive bunching of fruit.
Whitby, Ontario, Canada,1995. ©Vincenzo Pietropaolo

Manuel González greeting his sister Beda on his return home.
Monte Prieto, Guanajuato, Mexico, 1994.
©Vincenzo Pietropaolo

EVOLVING TRIANGULATIONS WITHIN THE ITALY-CANADA-UNITED STATES BORDERLANDS

Luisa Del Giudice

My daughter, pursuing her Ph.D. in environmental studies, provided what was, for me, a novel metaphoric handle for this exploration, when she explained that "triangulation" is the basic tool by which cartographers establish their bearings, and that a minimum of three points was required for navigation (see Figure 1). That sounded appropriate to my own three-point navigations. Yes, I could use this metaphor. First, my mother, two sisters and I had indeed navigated on a sea-faring transatlantic ship from the Italian port of Naples, to Halifax, Canada in the dead of winter, 1956. And as an ethnographer/folklorist, I could also point to our disciplinary assumption that research implies some form of "journey of discovery" (frequently to fieldwork destinations in distant lands). Among the earliest Italian Canadians, pride of place could go to Giuseppe Francesco Bressani,[1] an Italian Jesuit sent to

---

[1] The Jesuit Father Francesco Giuseppe Bressani, an Italian missionary born in Rome in 1612, spent several years in Québec ministering to the French, then to the Alonquin and Huron. After being captured and tortured by the Iroquois, he spent most of his time at the missionary outpost, Sainte Marie Among the Hurons, until its destruction by the Iroquois. In 1650, Bressani returned to Italy. He died in Florence in 1672. Bressani's *Breve Relatione d'alcune Missioni... nella Nuova Francia* (*Jesuit Relations*, Macerata 1653) can be considered the precursor of Italian Canadian writing. A biennial literary prize in his name was instituted in 1986 by the Italian Cultural Centre Society of Vancouver: the F. G. Bressani Literary Prize, on the occasion of Vancouver's Centennial and the launch of the First National Conference of Italian Canadian Writers. For an English edition and translation of Bressani's account, see Francesco Guardiani (ed.),

New France in the early 17th Century and thus has been considered the first Italian Canadian writer. Bressani was a Jesuit and *voyageur*, ethnographer of the Huron and Algonquins, and a writer—all rolled into one.

I continued to explore the issue of voyages and personal geo-cultural positioning. I continued the exercise in metaphorical thinking, inspired by the number 3. I became obsessed with triangles, explored diverse triangles, and considered many sorts of triangular identities. Some triangles were near and some farther afield. What did I discover? I learned that triangles could be both good and bad. In politics, triangulation had recently come to be associated with Bill Clinton, ever positioning himself between Right and Left. In family psychology, triangulation referred to family dysfunctionality and indirection (in the vernacular, for example: "playing one parent off the other"). But, because I tended to identify with the positive side of geographic triangles, I focused on good triangles, on those closer to home, and on triangles with further metaphorical possibilities.

Regarding the physical stability of three, I remembered a film clip in *I Build the Tower*, a documentary on the Watts Towers (Byer and Landler 2006), in which Buckminster Fuller reflects on how the visionary artist, Sabato (Sam) Rodia had intuited the absolute natural stability of the triangle and thereby constructed his feat of intuitive engineering (the tallest Tower being 99 ½ feet of reinforced concrete, all on a base of 14 inches),

---

Francesco Giuseppe Bressani, *Breve relatione d'alcune missioni dei PP. della Compagnia di Giesù nella Nuova Francia*, Toronto: Legas, 2011. (From: http://www.thecanadianencyclopedia.ca/en/article/francesco-giuseppe-bressani-literary-prize/).

by essentially compiling triangles. I reflected on this solid foundation of three from my own tripartite approach to personal and professional life, as I had finally achieved greater equilibrium by balancing: brain, heart, and hands; that is: thinking, feeling, doing; and thus: scholarship, spirituality, social action. This achievement of a balanced, complex but three-dimensional way of life, was essential and attractive to me, and had been achieved at the great cost of life-long learning, as well as trial and error.

But quite beyond such metaphorical propensities, in my own field of ethnography—but not limited to this discipline—triangulation refers to multi-directional and multi-methodological approaches, whereby one seeks to corroborate findings by using different data sets and frames of analysis (see Figure 2). In oral historical research, I had used the term to refer to the process of contextualizing the personal interview by referring to historic, socio-economic, and cultural parameters, in order to properly situate and understand what was being observed and described (Del Giudice 2009a).

I will here situate myself geographically, according to a sort of Global Positioning System, by identifying my own specific triangulation: I was born in Terracina (prov. of Latina), in Central Italy, emigrated as an infant, with my mother and two sisters in the mid-1950s to Toronto, returned to Italy in my early twenties to study Italian Medieval and Renaissance literature at the University of Florence, then relocated to Los Angeles for a doctorate in Italian Literature in 1981—which ironically, at that furthest remove on the Pacific shore —returned me to my family's Italian peasant and migrant world in a profound way, with a dissertation on folksong (the fieldwork for which straddled regional Italy: from the Appennino Pavese, to Terracina, and several regional sources in Toronto). This *volte-face* pointed me towards new scholarly destinations with a specific socio-political mission,[2] that is, to listen to ancestral voices in order to reconstruct, for myself personally and for my generation, basic knowledge about Italian oral culture and oral history. It also, in time, led to situating my scholarly work in public, as well as in academic, settings—at least insofar as far as this was possible, given the general hostility or indifference toward this material in Italian academia. I even went so far as to found the public nonprofit Italian Oral History Institute (IOHI) in order to accomplish the task.

Was my commitment to the culture of my Toronto cohort a case of "distance making the heart grow fonder"? A way of bringing that world closer to mine on the Pacific coast? Of making certain I would need to return again and again for family visits *and* scholarly research? Perhaps. But if nothing else, distance gave me perspective, helped me to see more clearly a broader context, and to discern the intimate reasons, no less than larger patterns, of movement, rapprochements, and distancing. It also helped me develop personal and other strategies for Italian cultural survival, transformation, and (re)use, in a sort of enhanced bricolage. Because I may have felt myself on many peripheries, geographic, social, and otherwise, I identified with (or at least did not shy away from) the margins—using the rhetoric of the margins, of disenfranchised

---

[2] For a more detailed account of this autobiographical journey, see: Del Giudice 2017.

voices, of invisibility—as have many scholars in a number of disciplines including those who work in diaspora (Italian and otherwise), folklore, feminist, ethnic studies, and oral history. Did these fields attract me *because* they studied the margins?

More recently, on the other hand, in our increasingly multi-centered, consciously globalized world, the very *topos* of marginality and of "outsider," may no longer serve, or at least, may have lost some of its efficacy. Any "margin" may be at the "center" of other networks, social and otherwise. We are all at the center of something, just as we are all on the margins of some other thing. In any case, there is power and strength in the so-called "margins," as so much recent scholarship in gender, race/ethnic, and postcolonial studies, has argued.[3] This marginal place/space enhances understanding (through personal experience) and there-by grants opportunities for bridging in compassionate action, solidarity, global reach, especially in peace and social justice settings. It also alerts us to the dynamics, dangers, and vulnerabilities of those who live on the disenfranchised margins, i.e., irregular migrants and refugees.

I began by briefly considering a few of the triangular and binary divides I've inhabited, but let me pause now to focus on how growing up in Toronto has strongly influenced my worldview and my scholarly work. First, Toronto is considered (for better or worse) the hegemonic Canadian city. The city also has the largest post-WWII Italian population in North America (over ½ million), with a significant portion of the entire

---

[3] My own contribution to this discourse, as it applies to academic and public work, and social advocacy within the Italian diaspora specifically, may be found in Del Giudice 2009b.

population represented by first-generation immigrants.[4] I grew up among other first-generation Italian dialect-speakers. My first Italian course at the University of Toronto was for dialect-speakers (*dialettofoni*). A significant component of my peers belonged to this Italian working-class minority group which—if not so vocal then—has increasingly found its voice, but always constituted a significant and visible part of the Toronto landscape. There was strength in numbers. And there was the ability to maintain many traditions and cultural ways, as well as a significant economic presence in a fast-developing city, much of it being constructed by Italians. It took a while (and distance) for me to recognize the empowering aspects of this egalitarian multiethnic and largely migrant milieu as a positive *civic* model, and to thereafter (and today) advocate for such a model—largely in the U.S.A. We needn't fear immigrants (working class and otherwise), as the current U.S. administration encourages us to do, but rather welcome them and then give them the opportunity to do what they do best: work and build and contribute.

---

[4] Confirmed by Donna Gabaccia (whom I thank profusely) via email communication, wherein she refers that: "Toronto is home to the fourth largest Italian population outside of Italy, behind São Paulo, Brazil, Buenos Aires, Argentina, and New York City, respectively. As of the Canada 2016 Census, there were 511,680 Italian Canadians located in the Greater Toronto Area […]. As of the 2000 census, 692,739 New Yorkers reported Italian ancestry, making them the largest European ethnic group in the city. In 2011, the American Community Survey found there were 49,075 persons of Italian birth in New York City […]. Assuming the number of Italian born in NY is accurate (and I have no reason to doubt it), then, yes those of Italian birth in Toronto far surpasses those in NYC."

Canada also offers educational opportunities to a wider segment of the population (newer immigrant included) than is accessible in the U.S.A., given the more segregated nature of education and of the social fabric more generally in the latter. Had I been raised in the U.S.A, and given my economic background, I surmise that I might not have stood much of a chance to pay the exorbitant tuition fees for admission to a first-rate university. I am forever grateful for my University of Toronto education—which would have been more affordable in any case, given that I was awarded a four-year merit scholarship to University College, which saw me through. Indeed, as I read about the crippling debt American college students incur for their educations today, I consider it nothing short of miraculous that after 11 years of university education (at the universities of Toronto, Florence, and Los Angeles), my grand total debt equaled $2,000 (CDN) in 1987! To say nothing of the health-care system which surely helped my ailing father, for example, live to the ripe old age of 84, despite his many health issues, including heart disease, requiring triple, and then quadruple bypass surgeries. He too was forever grateful to Canada, and felt no nostalgia for Italy or for any return. By virtue of such personal experiences in Canada and Italy, some "triangulars" in these borderlands, such as myself, have tended to become advocates for universal education, healthcare, and immigration reform in the U.S; that is, such a triangulation has directly influenced our social as well as political tendencies.

It was though, the specific milieu of 1960s and 1970s Italian Toronto, which significantly marked my own sense of Italian culture and my eventual realignment with ethnographic and oral historical research, as vocation. Frankly, why more scholars with similar experiences had *not* aligned themselves with their own Italian culture, remains a mystery to me. To be fair though, I was merely fortunate to have encountered Folklore and Mythology, Ethnomusicology, and Oral History as formal areas of scholarship at the University of California, Los Angeles (UCLA). Italian Departments, in my experience, were generally limiting, colonial outposts, sometimes politically unenlightened, defending their narrow literary canon, and simply had not given us the tools to do this sort of work nor to ask these sorts of questions. Although, it was not universally so throughout the diaspora, as I have since learned, upon reviewing the recent book *Italian Music in Australia*, but professors such as Antonio Comin have been few and far between.[5]

Geographic distance from Toronto and Italy, constant cultural triangulating, travel between the United States, Canada, and Italy, and a new scholarly focus which required direct field research in all three places, led to a personal connection with active global scholarly networks. All of this helped me develop a sense of critical resistance (and a network of resistance) to mainstream models of Italian Studies, as well as confidence to pursue an alternative, non-literary model—despite the disadvantages of working largely on the outside, beyond the pale of institutional support and recognition. Things have changed as a record of publi-

---

[5] In my pre-publication book review of *Italian Music in Australia* (Barwick and Sorce Keller 2013), included in the published volume itself (entitled "Parallel Universes"), I reflected on Antonio Comin's life work within the University of Flinders, which caused me to ask myself the "what could have been" questions had such efforts been made within academia during my own university years in Canada.

cation, organization, international experience, and social advocacy has given me wider exposure and credibility.

My twenty formative years in Toronto continue to resonate throughout my life and work as I continue to return to my family of 3 sisters, their families, and my mother who live there and with whom I have maintained close ties. In the early years of my absence, I returned only to visit family, but later Canada became enmeshed in my professional scholarly life as well.[6] At first, I incorporated fieldwork in Toronto into my Ph.D. fieldwork. My earliest folklore fieldwork took place during the mid-1980's (funded by a Multicultural Directorate grant) to investigate traditional song culture among immigrants. It continued with subsequent self-funded research on architecture, faith healers, wine cellars, and food utopias among Italian Canadians (http://luisadg.org/wp/about-2/). I focused on the cultural practices and worldview of peasant-derived Toronto Italians; and later did the same for peasant culture in Italy (from narrative ballads in the north to *neo-tarantismo* in the south), later still in the U.S.A, shuttling to and fro between the three culture zones, thereby bringing knowledge and direct experience of the three to bear on my understanding of all these topics, all from a triangulated perspective. My work increasingly evolved toward auto-ethnography, as I reflect, write,

---

[6] Only about a decade or so ago, did it occur to me to re-trace the triangle *in reverse*, that is, back to Canada, re-crossing the border *as* a scholar, via lectures, conferences (York Univ., Univ. of Toronto, the Canadian Society for Italian Studies, IASA in Toronto, Italian Canadian Archives conference at the University of Guelph), reporting on Italian Canadian research, and on the independent ethnographic and oral historical scholarly path I had traveled.

and present this native, assimilated, and transformed peasant culture in my own way. My world and work is that of cross-continental folk revivalism and advocacy, more or less "in synch" with Italians in Italy, and within other Italian diasporas. That is, the world to which I have devoted my professional energies has been, on the one hand, remembering, documenting, adapting and transforming; and on the other, resisting and advocating. But whereas, I had previously often *felt* afar, an outsider, marginal, today I know such work responds to current sensibilities, as we strive toward living within rooted cultures of our own, while creating alternative worldviews which value progressive, egalitarian, and more democratic notions of culture and life. Distances have become drastically compressed thanks to social media, allowing us to stay focused and globally connected around issues we share across diasporas—wherein margins and boundaries seem to disappear.[7] Today, I feel well poised for the challenges of a globalized world. I embrace that world.

How has my Italian, Italian Canadian, and Italian American scholarship worked out for me, as a resident

---

[7] Since giving this paper in 2014, the diasporas have met once again, not only on Facebook and other social media as they had been doing for years prior, but formally and in person--another example of the ongoing communication between diasporas that have occurred at conferences and meetings on migrations for years. I am referring to the three-phase diasporic conferences in: Melbourne (April 4-8, 2018), New York (Nov 1-3, 2018), and Genova (June 27-29, 2019), another important initiative whereby the diaspora is meeting itself *in* the diaspora, as well as in Italy (see: *Diaspore Italiane: Italy in Movement*, https://www.diasporeitaliane.com/). I presented "Beating the Drum: Italian Traditional Music Advocacy in the Diaspora" (https://www.youtube.com/watch?v=zVEE6yo79Gw) at the Melbourne meeting, and attended the second meeting at the Calandra Institute, by chance, thanks to my simultaneously-occurring resident research fellowship.

of Los Angeles since 1981? Los Angeles is one of the most cosmopolitan places on earth, a frontier for innovation and creativity, a fairly open and liberating milieu for the many who have continued to come to work and live there. As for fellow-Canadians in southern California, I learned the interesting factoid (at a Canadian Consul's University of Toronto Alumni gathering back in the 1990s) that "Los Angeles was Canada's fifth largest city"![8] I was not exactly sure if it was offered in jest, but it sounded credible. (Similar claims have been made for many other ethnic and national groups in Los Angeles: i.e., that our city housed the largest group of Armenians outside Armenia's national borders; had the largest numbers of Native Americans in the country, and so forth). I too had met so many closeted Canadians (even Italian Canadians) in Los Angeles, that the claim did not seem extravagant. Statistics confirm that the largest number of immigrants from Canada were in California and Florida—California leading by about

---

[8] The states with the largest number of immigrants from Canada are California and Florida. According to Census 2000, California had the largest number of foreign born from Canada (141,181), followed by Florida (99,139). The remaining 10 states with the largest numbers of immigrants from Canada included New York (54,876), Michigan (49,515), Washington (47,568), Massachusetts (40,247), Texas (36,802), Arizona (26,323), Illinois (19,098), and Connecticut (19,083). One in every 10 non-immigrants admitted as temporary workers, exchange visitors, and intracompany transferees in the United States was from Canada. According to Department of Homeland Security data for fiscal year 2002, 133,367 or 10.3 percent of the nearly 1.3 million nonimmigrants admitted as temporary workers, exchange visitors, and intracompany transferees in the United States were foreign-born Canadians. http://www.migrationpolicy.org/article/foreign-born-canada-united-states#4 (accessed Oct. 3/14). It would be interesting to note how these numbers have changed before and since the Trump presidency.

50% (according to Census 2000, of the 141,181 Canadians living in U.S., 99,139 were in California. I doubt these numbers account for those "transiting," here as impermanent migrants, as so many continue to be, especially in Los Angeles (e.g., particularly in "the [Entertainment] Industry").[9] It would be interesting to check the figures as of the last U.S. presidential election, given the hostile anti-migration sea-change it has ushered in, even as concerns "friendly" neighbors. But Canadians have headed south as "snow birds" (wintering in warmer climes), as short-term tourists, or for employment, for decades, and likely longer. Bitter winters account for the first cohort, and employment opportunities for the second. The employment opportunities however, have been reciprocal, varying according to economic sector. But as far as Canadian winters are concerned, I've long been convinced that you could simply show a Canadian a palm tree and s/he would follow you anywhere (especially to Florida or California)!

For this southern Italian Canadian American (as it has for many Italians), the Mediterranean milieu of California seems to provide greater natural affinities, allowing for more expressions of our Mediterranean roots via agriculture, viticulture, and architecture, than is generally the case in other regions of North America. This environmental fact alone has had repercussions on my work. It partly brought me to, but thereafter

---

[9] A Toronto nephew was so peeved at American cultural imperialism that for many years as a young adult, he sent me the ignored "secret" Canadian identity of many Hollywood celebrities… A 2014 Canadian stamp devoted to well-known Canadian comics, seems to underscore this need in the Canadian psyche: https://www.vistastamps.com/itm/canada-stamp-2772-great-canadian-comedians-4-25-2014!

certainly kept me in, southern California (strongly seconded by marriage and thereafter family). Furthermore, it had a significant impact on food-related scholarship and public-sector work, including Slow Food and the *Accademia Italiana della Cucina*. After all, southern California, and Los Angeles in particular, form a Mediterranean food mecca on the West coast.

The geographic triangulation whose virtues I have just extolled however, has also taken its existential toll: in feelings of restlessness, homelessness (or, effectively, an elusive and multi-centered sense of "home")—personal and professional—and the constant search for community belonging. For years, while living in Los Angeles, after it became clear that I was not going to be settling elsewhere, I continued to feel as though I was just passing through (to the dismay of my young family), and needed to develop some ways of feeling more rooted. As I came slowly to realize I was going to be permanently living in the city, raising a family, I was terrified by the prospect of stasis. Happily, I adapted. Los Angeles, is, of course, a transient's paradise, transience seemingly being the very essence of the city. Did anyone intentionally settle in Los Angeles, I wondered? Luckily though, I was able to continue my wandering ways, and not even early motherhood stopped me from traveling widely (mostly for professional reasons). Sometimes I took children with me, as I did on early fieldwork trips to Italy. But mostly, I was able to leave them in my husband's and our babysitter's care. I am eternally grateful for my enlightened, professionally-supportive, and economically-stable husband—all of which attributes allowed me the rare privileges of frequent travel and commitment to areas of study which were not institutionally-supported in our neck of the woods.

Nonetheless, triangulation has proven quite challenging, professionally-speaking. For a variety of reasons, finding *institutional* homes in which to practice my trade of folklore and oral history proved so difficult that I had to build my own: the I.O.H.I. As a naturally thrifty soul, I was able to do much with so little, and to *arriangiarmi,* in order to salvage a semblance of a professional identity. We Italians are, after all, homebuilders are we not? I learned to build mine. Rather than diasporic dispersal leading to fragmentation, I keenly resisted, realizing I could simply inhabit *all* those places simultaneously. One might go and return, time and time again, spinning out across the world in international conferences, teaching, and continuing research. And all the while, I reflected on these triangulations, edited volumes, assembled a collegial family in many different places—although the scholars with whom I most closely share interests remain those in the Mediterranean Section of the American Folklore Society.

Further, this existential triangle has made me fairly alert to socio-linguistic "code switching," and to the issue of an ever-vigilant negotiation of cultural identities as I situate or position myself within the triangulation at any specific moment. Of course, one aspires to keeping all points in equipoise (=equilateral triangle), and to achieving one's steady bearings—even though I find myself increasingly favoring shifts toward a fourth or fifth point, branching out in search of increased global "citizenship." Triangles can thus become many-sided polygons, as I create personal and professional networks, over and over again, in order to achieve change from within, aiming for over-arching paradigm shifts.

Another strategy in service to larger social justice is to link, wherever possible, and from whichever vantage point we may be inhabiting our specific knowledge to address broader issues. In my case, I intentionally choose traditions and customs from Italian-rooted culture to reach toward that global reality, applying my scholarship and organizational skills to call attention to urgent, current issues of human rights and social justice. For example, individual creativity and community embrace (Watts Towers); welcoming the stranger and feeding the poor (St. Joseph's Tables); truth and reconciliation (anti-Columbus Campaign). Viewed in retrospect, I have little doubt that the existential state of being "betwixt and between" helped me choose my very topics of research, interpretative tendencies, and public programs. St. Joseph's Tables represent an excellent custom, taken from the Italian and Italian (Sicilian) cultural diaspora itself, of practicing hospitality and food justice. But in order to make its largest impact in a diaspora context, it requires reaching beyond the insular and embracing cultural crossings—all of which must be learned, practiced, and perfected. The destitute are no longer Italians, for the most part, but immigrants such as Italians had been just that, decades and a century earlier, and should be encouraged to remember, to cultivate empathy, and to become allies to more recent arrivals. In recent oral historical research, I found visionary working-class Sabato (Sam, Simon) Rodia, the so-called "outsider" artist of the Watts Towers. As a marginalized and reviled southern Italian living during a period of acute hostilities toward this ethnic group in America, his response was one of intense creativity, extraordinary art, and a communal embrace as he opened his arms to all those around him, in the monument which he named: *Nuestro Pueblo*. His own practice allows us to call forth the values of personal creativity to overcome hardships, and the ability of our art to create community and common ground. That is what the Watts Towers Common Ground Initiative seeks to do in ever widening circles. And, as a last example of the whys and wherefore of my scholarship, as it relates to triangular worlds and social issues, from the beginning of my folklore studies, the very *raison d'être* of those studies, has represented an amplification of the spoken and sung word (that is, oral culture) over written, literary culture, of dialects over standard Italian, local traditions over national culture, the many and diverse against the orthodox, dogmatic, and uniform. Such was the intimate Italian culture I had experienced personally in all my years in Toronto, which also expressed the social class to which we belonged. It was the impulse to understand that world which led to more formal study, thereby helping me to learn about the historic injustices and silencing endured by an entire class of peasants-turned-diaspora Italians. Yes, in some odd way, this discipline, these specific areas of study, both derived from (and amplified) my/our own sense of being unheard, unseen, ever-marginalized *outsiders*. Further, gender certainly amplified this existential state still further, as I experienced it. I was a female scholar of Italian folk culture and oral history in a largely male academic world of Italian literary scholars. I experienced a reluctance of that establishment to partner with me, that is with (pardon the modesty) an articulate, well-educated (and published) female director of a successful non-profit educational organization exquisitely poised between academic and public sector—ideals being touted at UCLA at that very time in history (i.e., "UCLA in LA"), an organization already achieving precisely that, and available to help one of its own departments also achieve such goals. But, alas, current well-known gender dynamics and power structures, increasingly revealed by the MeToo movement, makes my specific case, in retrospect, laughably ordinary. At the time however, the pain was acute and devastating, and rejection baffling. It is a small comfort to learn today of all the strategies used against women I had not then identified, but that have since been made abundantly clear, thanks to the testimony of so many women. I mourn all the capable women, their unrealized (or not fully-realized) talent, fallen by the wayside, often thanks to entrenched and gender-biased systems of exclusion. Our grief rises up in one muffled cry. On the other hand, strategies and determination learned from my hard-driving immigrant father, taught me to persist, to resist, to continue along my path and to survive however best I could.

I am not comfortable with walls and with hierarchies: national walls, social divisions, tribalisms (especially Italian), even barriers between academic workers (i.e., professors, adjuncts, independent scholars, that is: those inside vs. those outside the hallowed walls; those with job security and those forever scrambling). This aversion runs deep. I have intentionally sought to create bridges over such divides, even risking censure and alienation from my own "tribe," at times, because I believe that this is what we must all seek to do: viz., act to promote peace, equity, justice. How does this play out? Let me offer a couple of examples: I aim to do good, even as I try to overcome the inevitable critics of "do goodism," learning to listen to those *outside* my own ethnic group, in the hopes that I might get it right and actually create strong bonds of trust and mutual respect, as well as become an ally. This has been the case with respect to the Italian/African American bridge around the Watts Towers, where my secondary (and triangular) goal was also to find a space for an Italian presence, to triangulate ethnically, and perhaps to also mediate between an earlier and a more recent migration in a place where the established African community and the later Latino influx had not always co-existed peacefully (see Del Giudice 2014). Another instance of boundary crossing is represented by an emerging Indigenous/Italian allyship, in a racial boundary crossing which I had not yet personally experienced. Together with scholars of Italian American history and culture, we circulated a national petition to suspend Columbus Day as a national holiday,[10] simultaneously circulating another, local petition to have the day renamed in Los Angeles as "Sabato Rodia Italian Heritage Day." On October 8, 2018, the first Indigenous Peoples Day in Los Angeles history took place. I not only helped celebrate the long-awaited new holiday but sat on a panel in the City Council Chambers, the very spot in which opposition between the Indigenous

---

[10] This campaign, spearheaded by me, Claudio Fogu, Laura Ruberto, and Joseph Sciorra, was primarily aimed at the Italian American Congressional Delegation: https://nocolumbusday.wordpress.com/about/.

(Mitch O'Farrell) and the Italian (Joseph Buscaino) Councilmen took place, to explain why, as an Italian American (and as an Italian Canadian), I supported Indigenous Peoples and their celebration, and why I did not support the Italian community rallying around a historic figure such as Columbus. I argued that, in any case, we had better heroes to celebrate, ones in closer touch with the actual experience of Italian immigrants, and certainly more atuned to issues of social equity and anti-colonialism. In Canada, for decades, we have been publically acknowledging the First Peoples' land we are on, as a routine ritual opening to many conferences, as well as other academic and public events. It seemed to me a modest sign of respect and justice that cost the settler peoples little but went some way (symbolically speaking) to acknowledging and affirming the rights and dignity of First Nation peoples. Of course, more tangible progress remains to be achieved. Our campaign especially sought to *not* continue the erasure, invisibility, and continuing oppression of Indigenous Peoples.

As for healing other sorts of historic wounds, as they specifically related to Italians, I considered my visiting professorship in Ethiopia—a graduate oral history seminar—a means of doing my small part of righting an Italian colonial-era wrong, and providing several key tools (physical, methodological, and theoretical) to help Ethiopians document their stories, their languages, their history. I was able to leave a video camera behind, along with other equipment for which I had been able to gather together funds in LA in order to provide my students at Addis Ababa University with research essentials. One may easily imagine how moved I was, when one student commented: "*Now*, we feel like true folklorists!" I took the opportunity to demonstrate interviewing techniques by interviewing the found-er of Fregenet, a foundation which funded an exemplary elementary school (and community center) in Addis (see: http://fregenetfoundation.org/), Tafesse Woubshet, who was in Addis, thereby exposing students to diaspora Ethiopians in their midst. A student and I visited the school, which led to my involvement with this L.A.-based Ethiopian diasporic foundation.

The concept of locating "home" and a community of belonging has been a life-long endeavor which requires constant (psychological) positioning and repositioning—as it does for all people in movement, in diasporas, whether of the forced or the "voluntary" sort. I have been dogged by such questions even before I ever left Toronto and embarked on my life-long habit of travel... In fact, the "Ugly Duckling" story was one of my defining inner narratives: if only I could find my *true* family, I'd finally feel at home. All adolescents perhaps experience such feelings of alienation, which propel them toward voyages of self-discovery. Mine seems to have been an extreme case. It never seems to have ended... Beginning at the turn of the new millennium, and after professional disappointments, I embarked once again on other sorts of inner journeys, pilgrimages, and explorations in various faith traditions, attempting to align more with a *spiritual* family and a *spiritual* home, which might accompany me everywhere, that I might feel at home anywhere. And so it has proven.

Further, to my delight, I found that community could be *created*, called into being from thin air, through *intentional* and focused efforts, and so I habitually created such communities—through Italian community programs, family dinners, friend gatherings, editing projects, women's circles, and even panel-organization. All of these were a means of invoking community to focus attention around a range of issues and practices, sometimes in intimate settings, and sometimes in public arenas, and frequently calling upon my personal triangle of Italy, Toronto, Los Angeles. Living profoundly in and through these many geographic and human sites has helped me understand and intimately situate myself, as I navigate between me, you, and us, remaining all the while in perpetual motion, feeling at "home" in multiples places, and with diverse people. Even an extremely diffuse and transient place such as Los Angeles has increasingly come to feel like home.

The need to stay in motion, however, especially within my own Italy-Canada-USA triangle, is profound and essential to my sense of self and sense of wellbeing. It consciously began in the late 1970s when I made an unprecedented (for my gender and cohort) move to Florence, Italy, to study for two years. I knew no one there and simply jumped into a new milieu. It represented a long period of distance from home, little-communication with family, and a solitary process of individuation. (It also initiated my next leap to the United States.) In my parents' eyes, perhaps only an educational justification (one focused on Italian studies, no less) could possibly have legitimated such a protracted journey away from home. But once my family accepted the fact that I intended to extend my education and become a scholar (whatever that might mean, they really had no idea), I was able to use that goal as rationale to justify further explorations away from my place of origin, in small incremental steps. Eventually, I moved to Los Angeles, California and never returned home to live close to my family of origin. That initial separation from home in the 1970s broke the spell. The tightly tethered ropes to family loosened, the distance increased, both proved critical to my project of self-knowing and knowing the world. Ironically, of course, that life-project returned me time and again to my very first and second departure points, as I tried to understand its culture, history, and diaspora, and to situate my place of origin and of belonging.

The distance also launched me into processes of intense self-reflection, of writing, and of unmoored self-reliance. Today, I consider myself an "extreme" independent scholar, completely institutionless, and free to academically wander, wherever I am called: from presenting Veterans History Project workshops in the Northern Mariana Islands, to lecturing in a Scottish ethnographic field school, to delivering a keynote in an Island Dynamics conference in China. The farther the field, the better. The need to be in motion has actually become more pervasive and deeply engrained, taking me far beyond my essential triangle. I seem to find it difficult to sit still (besides the sitting required for writing, but today, even that...) And although I remain a proponent of stillness (proscribed in the art of "spiritual direction," see Del Giudice 2009b), I seem to favor walking, swimming, in short, various sorts of *moving* meditations. I engage in frequent peregrinations, pilgrimages, even in my own city of Los Angeles—documenting landscapes, people, and places as I go. The latest adventure on this front, took me to Santiago de

Compostela, Spain, and its Camino. Facebook has become my constant companion as I share journeys, encounters, sightings, and reflections. But I have traveled around the globe, mostly for professional reasons. I tend to say "yes" to the opportunities which have come my way, especially the unexpected and rare ones. But even those closer at hand intrigue me. During the summer of 2014, I took my second cross-continent road trip (Toronto–Oregon–California) with the daughter mentioned at the beginning of this essay. In her Oregon State University research vehicle, with a canoe latched on top (a perfect Canadian icon perhaps: see Figure 3), we embarked on what I imagined to be a replication, in part, of the Canadian *voyageur*'s western routes of discovery along the French River (see Figures 4 and 5). I enjoyed the symbolic value of our route, retracing this exploratory journey.

My friends, family, and colleagues know that I love *to go* and are often astounded at the places which show up in my Facebook feed, never quite knowing where I'll be next. I no longer ask the question of where I might belong because I suspect the answer to remain gnomic: everywhere, nowhere, somewhere in between, or better yet: *on the road*—with a camera and notebook in hand. I have even fantasized my next project to be something in the line of "Notes from the Road," a not-so-unusual travel genre, after all. Or perhaps, I could merely focus on Images from the Road—that is, fewer words and more photography. I seem to be happiest when traveling anywhere, particularly if I have never been there before, and I feel most lucid when I am between places, reflecting on *there* while I am *here*; or *here* while I am *there*. I'll confess that I recently applied for an AmTrak writer's grant that would have allowed me to write while traveling on a train, a perfect enactment of the thinking-while-on-the-move paradigm. Unfortunately, too many other authors had similar yearnings, so I did not receive the award. I seem to be more mentally alert while away from my own home, writing in one coffeehouse or library after another (although never the same one for very long). Once I have become an *habituée*, the work becomes harder. Home in some ways, has become synonymous with my portable laptop computer.

But such restlessness might also represent an expression of some deeper malaise. In brief, what are some of the downsides, I might mention? Feelings of exclusion. The realization that no point or group on my triangle, and least of all Italian Canadians, had paid much attention to their own diaspora of colleagues abroad nor to their writings (I'm certain they would note a similar sense of neglect). Italians, on the other hand, recently discovering that they have their own buried emigrant past, are barely coming to terms with an entire, substantial group of scholars who have been engaged in studying the Italian diaspora for decades. Being an institutionally-free transnational has provided other challenges, of course, even though I have come to embrace my own peculiar state, and its positive aspects, as a free-floating, multiple citizen, and Independent Scholar, equal parts Italian, Italian Canadian, California-Italian—that is, a scholar simultaneously inside and outside, both embraced and excluded, forging forth, nonetheless, as a one-woman band, banging on my own little Facebook drum about the things I do which concern me most, keenly listening for what comes next, and sometimes leading the way.

WORKS CITED

Bressani 1653. Francesco Giuseppe Bressani, *Breve relatione d'alcune missioni dei PP. della Compagnia di Giesù nella Nuova Francia* (ed. Francesco Guardiani. Toronto: Legas, 2011).

Del Giudice 2009a: "Speaking Memory: Oral History, Oral Culture and Italians in American," in *Oral History, Oral Culture and Italian Americans* (selected papers from the 38th AIHA annual meeting, Los Angeles, 2005), ed. Luisa Del Giudice, New York: Palgrave Macmillan. 3-18.

_____. 2009b. "Ethnography and Spiritual Direction: Varieties of Listening," in *Rethinking the Sacred*, Proceedings of the Ninth SIEF (Société Internationale d'Ethnologie et Folklore) Conference in Derry 2008, ed. by Ulrika Wolf-Knuts, Department of Comparative Religion, Åbo Akademi University, Religionsvetenskapliga skrifter: 9-23.

_____. 2013. "Parallel Universe," in Linda Barwick and Marcello Sorce Keller (eds.), *Italy in Australia's Musical Landscape*, Lyrebird Press. 3-14

_____. 2013. *Italian Music in Australia* (Barwick and Sorce Keller 2013).

_____. 2014. "Feeding the Poor — Welcoming the Stranger: The Watts Towers Common Ground Initiative and St. Joseph's Communal Tables in Watts," in Regina Bendix and Michaela Fenske (eds.), *Political Meals (Politische Mahlzeit). Wissenschaftsforum Kulinaristik* (Forum Culinaristics), Lit-Verlag, 2014: 53-65.

_____. 2017. "Introduction: A Convocation of Wise Women and Reflections on Lives of Learning," 1-39 and "Making Dead Bones Sing: Practicing Ethnography in the Italian Diaspora," 140-170, in *On Second Thought: Learned Women Reflect on Profession, Community, and Purpose, Sault Lake City:* University of Utah Press.

———. 2020."Beating the Drum: Italian Traditional Music Advocacy in the Diaspora, in *Street Music and Narrative Traditions*, ed. by Sergio Bonanzinga, Luisa Del Giudice, Thomas McKean, Palermo: *Suoni e Cultura.*

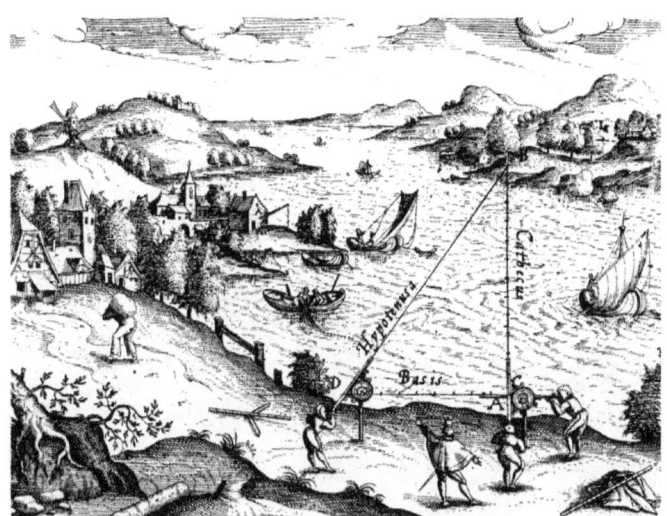

Figure 1. Illustration by Levinus Hulsius (1550 – 1606), German librarian, writer, public notary, editor, printer, and etcher. He was also a maker of scientific instruments, a linguist and lexographer.

Figure 2. Triangulations in design seems to capture best in visual form the increased knowing and "sight" that comes from this methodology. Photo credit: tomsturm-Fotolia.

Figure 3. On a Westward road trip, from Michigan to Oregon, to return the research vehicle my daughter, Elena Tuttle, had employed in a Great Lakes survey project with her Ph.D. director, Professor Dennis Albert.

Figure 4 and 5. Following the French River journeys of the Canadian *voyageurs*.

Contributors

LUISA DEL GIUDICE, Ph.D. is an Independent Scholar, former university academic (visiting professor at the University of California Los Angeles, and at Addis Ababa University, Ethiopia), public sector educator (Founder-Director of the Italian Oral History Institute), and community activist. She has published and lectured widely on Italian and Italian American and Canadian folklife, ethnology, oral history, and has produced many innovative public programs on Italian, Mediterranean regional and folk culture, and local history, both in Los Angeles and in Italy. Among the publications she has edited or written are: *Cecilia: testi e contesti di un canto narrativo tradizionale* (Brescia: Grafo); *Studies in Italian American Folklore* (Logan: Utah UP); *Imagined States: Nationalism, Utopia, and Longing in Oral Cultures* (Logan: Utah UP); *Performing Ecstasies: Music, Dance, and Ritual in the Mediterranean* (Ottawa: Institute for Medieval Music); *Oral History, Oral Culture and Italian Americans* (NY: Palgrave); *Sabato Rodia's Towers in Watts: Art, Migrations, Development* (NY: Fordham UP); *On Second Thought: Learned Women Reflect on Profession, Community, Purpose* (Salt Lake City: U of Utah Press); Forthcoming: *In Search of Abundance: Paesi di Cuccagna and Other Gastronomic Utopias* (Bordighera).

GIOVANNA P. DEL NEGRO is Associate Professor of English at Texas A&M University. Her books include *Looking Through My Mother's Eyes: Life Stories of Nine Italian Immigrant Women in Canada* (Guernica, 2003, 1997) and *The Passeggiata and Popular Culture in an Italian Town: Folklore and the Performance of Modernity* (McGill-Queen's University Press, 2005), which was awarded the Elli Köngäs- Maranda prize by the Women's Section of the American Folklore Society. She is co-author of *Identity and Everyday Life: Essays in the Study of Folklore, Music and Popular Culture* (Wesleyan University Press, 2005) and past co-editor of the *Journal of American Folklore*. Her work explores issues of gender, ethnicity, and performance in both face-to-face interactions and mass-mediated forms of communication. Her current research focuses on the YouTube videos of "Nonna Maria's Cantina Canadese," and "Je m'appelle Guy, and I am not Canadian." Her publications on gender, assimilation, and whiteness in the party records of three Jewish women comics of the post-WWII era have appeared in several venues, including *A Jewish Feminine Mystique,* (Littman Library, 2010) and *Jews at Home,* (Brandeis University Press, 2010) and her piece on the sexual non-conformity and camp humor of Judy Tenuta is forthcoming in *Gender and Humor: Interdisciplinary and International Perspectives* (Routledge, 2014). She also has a chapter on the representation of Jewish women in the films of Woody Allen in an edited volume titled *Woody on Rye* (Brandeis University Press, 2013) and serves as a board member of "Media, Culture and the Arts," a book series of Lexington Books, a division of Rowman and Littlefield.

PASQUALE VERDICCHIO is a founding member of the Association of Italian Canadian Writers. He has published a number of books of translation and his own poetry through Guernica Editions and other presses. His most recent publications from Guernica include *This Nothing's Place* (winner of the 2010 Bressani Prize for Poetry), and *Fosfeni,* a translation of poetry by Andrea Zanzotto (2010). His essays on poetry, film, and literature have appeared in journals in North America and Europe. In 2011 Fairleigh Dickinson University Press published *Looters, Photographers, and Thieves: Topics in Italian Photographic Culture in the Nineteenth and Twentieth Centuries.* Verdicchio has taught literature, film and writing at the University of California, San Diego, since 1986.

INDEX

1964, 34
1994, 34

Abruzzo, 4, 7, 15, 16
Accademia Italiana della Cucina, 53
Adaptation, 30
Addis Ababa, Ethiopia, 59, 71
African Americans, 1, 11, 58
Afro-Metis Canadian, 10
Aggies, 16
Albert, Dennis, 68
Algonquin Indians, 42
American Folklore Society, 54
AmTrak Writer's Grant, 64
Appadurai, Arjun, 9
Appennino Pavese, vii, 44
Arizona, Canadians in (Census 2000), 51
Armenians, 51
Assimilation, 31

Belanger St. (Montreal), 12
Belgium, 4, 6, 7, 16
Bloomington, 16
Botkin, Benjamin, 2
Bowling Green, Ohio, 2, 16
Bressani, F.G., 41, 42
Bressani, F.G. Literary Prize, 41, 42
Breton, Raymond, 13
Buscaino, Joseph, 59

Calandra, John D. Calandra Italian American Institute, ix, 50,
California, vi, vii, 15, 17, 48, 51, 52, 53, 62, 63, 64
Canadians in California (Census 2000), 51

University of California, Los Angeles (UCLA), 48, 57
Canada, 3, 8, 35
Canadian Consul (of Los Angeles), 51
Canadian Society of Italian Studies (CSIS), 49
Castel, France, 5
CBC (Canadian Broadcasting Corporation), 13
Celentano, Adriano, 6
Census (2000), 52
Centro Donne, 18
CFA (Come From Away), 12, 14, 15, 26
China, conference in, 62
C.I.B.L. 104 Radio, 18
Cinquetti, Gigliola, 7
Clifford, James, 9
Clinton, Bill, 42
Collective Remembering, 38
College Station, Texas, 16, 17
Columbus, anti-Columbus Campaign, 55, 58, 59
Comin, Antonio, 48
Community, vii, 2, 5, 6, 15, 18, 28, 34, 36, 53, 55, 56, 58, 59, 60, 65
Communal, 37, 56, 65
Comparative, 34, 65
Conca d'Oro, 12
Connecticut, Canadians in (Census 2000), 51
Connections, 36
Content, vii, 33
Context, viii, 2, 14, 15, 21, 23, 26, 31, 32, 37, 43, 44, 55
Coordinates, 32, 36, 37
Cosmopolitan, 6, 7, 25, 26

Culture, 36
  Cultural Imaginary, 37
  Cultural Objects, 36
  Cultural Practices, 36
  Cultural Production, 31
  Cultural Coordinates, 36
  Displaced Culture, 36
Cultural Studies, 19
  Hegemonic Culture, 37
    Hegemonic Canadian City, 45

Danero, 5
Del Giudice, Luisa, v, 41, 43, 44, 45, 58, 62, 64, 65
Del Negro, Giovanna, v, vi, vii, 1, 4, 26, 27
Department of Homeland Security, 51
Devils in Paradise, 30
Dialogue, 34
Diaspora, vii, viii, ix, 26, 27, 45, 48, 50, 55, 56, 60, 61, 62, 64, 66; See: Sicilian Cultural Diaspora
Diaspore Italiane: Italy in Movement (conference), 50
Diouf, Mamadou, 11
Discovery, 32
Dolci, Roberto, ix
Diverse, 13, 31, 34, 42, 56, 60
  Diversity, 25, 34
Diversion, 33
Documentation, 37

Elaboration, 32
Essential, 16, 25, 26, 36, 43, 60, 61, 62,
Ethiopia, 60
Ethnomusicology (UCLA), 48

Evolution, evolving, vii, viii, 34, 37, 41
Existential, 36

Facebook, 50, 63, 64
Fermin, 35
F.I.L.E.F., 12, 18
Filmmaker, 33
First Generation, viii, 23, 31, 46
First Peoples, 59
Flinders, University of (Australia), 48
Florence, 41, 43, 47, 61,
  University of Florence, 43
Florida (Canadians in Census 2000), 51, 52
Fogu, Claudio, 59
Folklore, 2, 4, 5, 20
Folklore and Mythology (UCLA), 47
Fregenet Foundation (Los Angeles, Addis Ababa), 60
French River, 63
Fuller, Buckminster, 42

Gagliardi, Alfredo, 36
Gans, Herbert, 23
Garbiulo, Giovanni, 34
Gaze, 35
Genova, Italy, 50
Global Positioning System (GPS), 43
Gramsci, Antonio, 30
Great Lakes, 68

Halifax, Nova Scotia, 41
Hannerz, Ulf, 6, 9
Harney, Robert F., 1
Harvest Pilgrims, 35, 36
  Harvest Season, 35
Hebert, Anne, 10
Historical
  Historicization, 38

Historic Discontinuity, 31
Historic Present, 32
Historic Record, 32
Huron Indians, 41, 42

I Build the Tower (film), Brad Byer and Edward Landler, 42
Identities, v, vi, vii, 38
Illinois, Canadians in (Census 2000), 51
Incantation, 33
Indigenous
Indigenous/Italian Allyship, 58
Indigenous Peoples Day, 58, 59
Inhabitation, 30
Interactive, 37
Inventory, 31
Iroquois Indians, 41
Island Dynamics, 62
Italian/African American, 58
  Italian American Congressional Delegation, 58
Italian American Studies Association (IASA), vi, 49
Italian Canadian Archives, 49
Italian Cultural Centre Society of Vancouver, 41
Italianità, 37
Italian Music in Australia, 48, 65
Italian Oral History Institute (IOHI), viii, 44, 54
Italian Studies, 26, 48, 49, 61
Italy, v, vi, vii, ix, 3, 4, 7, 8, 10, 11, 14, 15, 26, 34, 41, 43, 44, 47, 48, 49, 50, 53, 61
Italians, vii, 6, 7, 8, 10, 11, 18, 24, 36, 46, 49, 52, 54, 55, 56, 59, 64
Italian Community, vii, 2, 15, 28, 34, 37, 58, 60,

Jedlowski, Paolo, 32
Jews, 2, 10
Jocardi , 9
John F. Kennedy High School (Montreal), 12

La Consolata Church (Montreal), 12
Lalonde, Michele, 24
La Presse, 9
Latino, influx into Watts, 58
Letter, 35
Los Angeles, California,
Los Angeles City Council, 58
  University of California, Los Angeles; See: California

Magic, 33
Massachusetts, Canadians in (Census 2000), 51
Medieval and Renaissance Literature , 43
Mediterranean, 26
Mediterranean Section of the American Folklore Society, 54
Melbourne (Australia), 50
Memories, 35
MeToo Movement, 57
Mexico, 35
Michigan, 68
Michigan (Canadians in Census 2000) 51
Migration, 7, 8, 28, 32, 36, 37, 50, 51, 57, 58

Emigration (out migration), 5, 7, 30, 31, 32, 57
   Post-emigrant, 30, 31
Immigrant, 1, 30 34
Immigration, 2, 8, 30, 47
   Anti-Immigration, 52
   Migrant Workers, 35
   Migrants, 28, 45, 52
Mina, 6
Minority, 31, 46
Montreal, Québec, 1, 4, 8, 10, 15, 16, 24, 34, 37
Movement
   MeToo, 57
   Separatist, 16, 36
Multicultural Directorate (Canada), 48

Naples, Campania, vii, 32, 41
   Napoletano, 33
Narration, 31, 32
   Narrative, 32, 33, 37, 49,
   Narratives, 31, 36, 40, 60, 65
   Narrative Strategies, 34
Narvaez, Peter, 13
National Conference of Italian Canadian Writers, 41
Native Americans, 51
Neo-tarantismo, vii, 49
Newfoundland, 3, 15, 16
New York (City), 46, 50
New York (state), Canadians in (Census 2000), 51
Non-hearing, 35
"Nonna Maria," viii, 70
North America, 14, 30, 31, 32, 45, 53
Northern Mariana Islands, 62
Nuestro Pueblo ("Watts Towers"), 56

O'Farrell, Mitch, 59
Oral History, vii, viii, 44, 45, 54, 57, 59
Oral History Program (UCLA), 48
Italian Oral History Institute, See: Italian
Oregon State University, 62
Ottawa, Canada, 15

Pacific Coast, 44
Pakistani, 10
"Parallel Universe," 48; See: *Italian Music in Australia*
Participatory, 31
Passeggiata, 4, 5, 6, 7, 8
Pate Chinois, 13
Patronato Italo-Canadese, 12
Pietropaolo, Vincenzo, 33, 37
Photography
   Photographer, 33
   Photographic, 36
Pilgrimage, 36, 37, See: Santiago de Compostela
Popular Culture, 2, 20
Post-WWII Italy, viii, 3, 6, 24, 45
Poutine, 13
Public Intellectual, 34, 37
Public Sphere, 37

Québec, vi, viii, 3, 10, 14, 15, 23, 24, 25, 33, 34, 41
Quiet Revolution, 3, 24

Recipes, 36
Recollection, 38
Regenerative, 31
Relationships, 38
Relative, 34
Residence, 37

Return, vi, viii, 6, 35, 36, 40, 42, 43, 44, 47, 48, 49, 54, 61, 62, 67
Rhyme, 32
Rhythm, 33
Ricordati di noi, 34, 36
Rodia, Sabato (Sam), "Sabato Rodia Italian Heritage Day," 58
Rome, 8, 15, 24, 41
Ruberto, Laura, vi, 59

Saint Finbar Elementary, 13
Saint John's, Newfoundland, vi, viii, 12, 14, 16
Saint Joseph's Tables, 55, 65
Saint Lawrence, 9
Sainte Marie Among the Hurons, 41
Saint Michel, 10, 12, 13
Salento, Puglia, vii
San Diego, California, vi, 32
San Remo, 6
Santiago de Compostela, Camino de, 63
Sciorra, Joseph, 59
Scottish Ethnographic Field School (University of Aberdeen), 62
Serra, Rosemary, ix
Sicilian Cultural Diaspora, 55
Slow Food, 53
Soundtrack, 35
Southern Question, 31
Storie comuni, 32
Stories, 27, 30, 32, 34, 59; See Narrative
Story, 32, 37, 60
Survival, 31
Cultural Survival, 44
Cultural Survivals, 4
Synch, 35

Tamburri, Anthony Julian, ix
Tana, Paul, 33, 37
Teledomenica, 34, 37
Television, 37
Tenuta, Judy, 2
Terracina, Lazio, vii, 43, 44
Testimony, 36
Testimonial, 37
Texas, 2, 16, 17, 20, 22, 26
Texas, Canadians in (Census 2000), 51
This Hour Has Twenty-Two Minutes, 14
Tim Hortons, 14
Toronto, Ontario, v, vi, viii, ix, 15, 36, 37, 43, 44, 45, 46, 47, 48, 49
University of Toronto, v, 46, 47, 51
Transitions, 36
Transnationalism, 64
Transnationalism and Identity, v, vi, ix
Transracial Adoption, 10
Triangulation, v, vii, ix, 30, 32, 36, 37, 41, 42, 43, 47, 53, 54, 66
Trudeau, Pierre Elliott, 3, 16
Trump, 51

UCLA, University of California Los Angeles, "UCLA in LA," 57
"Ugly Duckling," 60
United States, ix, 7, 10, 41, 46, 48, 51, 61
University
St. John's University, Newfoundland: See St. John's
University College (University of Toronto), 47

University of California,
    Los Angeles: See: Los
    Angeles
University of California,
    San Diego: See San
    Diego
University of Florence,
    See: Florence
University of Toronto,
    See: Toronto
York University
    (Toronto), 49
Valenziano, Anna, 35
Vancouver, British
    Columbia, vi, 29, 32,
    41
Vancouver, Italian Cultural
    Centre Society of, 41
Vellucci, Sabrina, ix
Verdicchio, Pasquale, v, vi,
    vii, ix, 30, 39
Veterans History Project, 62
Voyageur, 42, 63, 69

Walsh, Mary, 14
Washington, Canadians in
    (Census 2000), 51
Watts Towers, 42, 55, 56,
    58
Watts Towers Common
    Ground Initiative, 56
Werbner, Pnini, 6
Werbner, Richard, 9
West, Mae, 12
Witness, 32, 37
    Witnessing, 37
Workers, 35
Woubshet, Tafesse, 60

York University, See:
    University

ROBERT VISCUSI
—1941-2020—

Robert Viscusi was fundamental to the development of Bordighera Press; to its journal *VIA: Voices in Italian Americana*, and to the book series *VIA* FOLIOS.

One of his many ground-breaking articles, "Breaking the Silence: Strategic Imperatives for Italian American Culture," opened the *VIA*'s inaugural issue. In like fashion, his keenly satiric, genial long poem, "An Oration upon the Most Recent Death of Christopher Columbus," was the stimulus for the founding our first book series, *VIA* FOLIOS.

In later years we also published his epic poem, *Ellis Island*, a collection of sonnets whose "Star Review" from *Publishers Weekly*, that closed as follows: "[T]he sonnets are far from uniform, at times manifesting as short stories, at other times as short bursts of philosophical inquiry or bursts of pure song. This is a new delicacy for aficionados of creative poetry and an anthem of sorts for those who—however far removed from immigration—occasionally feel displaced from home."

ROBERT VISCUSI ESSAYS SERIES

Named in honor of the work of Robert Viscusi, this referred series is dedicated to the long essay. It intends to publish studies that are longer than the traditional journal-length essay and yet shorter than the traditional book-length manuscript. All books are peer-reviewed.

Linda L. Carroll. *Thomas Jefferson's Italian and Italian-Related Books in the History of Universal Personal Rights. An Overview.* Volume 1.

www.ingramcontent.com/pod-product-compliance
Lightning Source LLC
Chambersburg PA
CBHW022118090426
42743CB00008B/901